Isaac Newton

Reluctant Genius

Isaac Newton

Reluctant Genius

D. C. Ipsen

ENSLOW PUBLISHERS, INC.

Bloy St. & Ramsey Ave.
Box 777
Hillside, N.J. 07205
U.S.A.

P.O. Box 38
Aldershot
Hants GU12 6BP
U.K.

Library of Congress Cataloging in Publication Data

Ipsen, D. C.
Isaac Newton, reluctant genius.

Bibliography: p.
Includes index.
Summary: A biography of the seventeenth-century English scientist who developed the theory of gravity, discovered the secret of light and color, and formulated the system of calculus.
1. Newton, Isaac, Sir, 1642-1727—Juvenile literature. 2. Physicists—Great Britain—Biography—Juvenile literature. 3. Physics—History—Juvenile literature. 4. Calculus—History—Juvenile literature. [1. Newton, Isaac, Sir, 1642-1727. 2. Scientists] I. Title.
QC16.N7I67 1985 509'.2'4 [B] [92] 85-1581
ISBN 0-89490-090-0

Printed in the United States of America

10 9 8 7 6 5 4 3 2 1

Illustration Credits:
Grantham Library, p. 10; Hebrew University of Jerusalem, p. 61; Lord Portsmouth and the Portsmouth Estates, p. 42; Master and Fellows of Trinity College, Cambridge, pp. 17, 84; Mount Wilson and Las Campanas Observatories, p. 55; *Newton's* Principia: *Motte's Translation Revised*, by Florian Cajori, University of California Press, 1960, pp. 40, 47; Palomar Observatory, p. 57; Royal Society, pp. 9, 27, 37.

Contents

Preface

Writing about the life and works of a scientist such as Newton presents a special problem. He was not content to carry each project of his long life to its end before starting the next. In fact, the three biggest accomplishments of his career all had their beginning in a few "miraculous years" and received his attention off and on for decades after. I have chosen to organize the book more around his works than around the events of his life, and so I carry him from youth to old age several times as I relate his various accomplishments and their place in the history of science.

Although I have paid more attention to Newton's works than to his life, I have still described the significant events of his not terribly eventful life, but not always in sequence. A brief chronology at the end of the book may help the reader appreciate the sequence and timing of those events.

I am indebted to Owen Gingerich, Professor of Astronomy and the History of Science at Harvard, and to Carl Ipsen, student in the History of the Exact Sciences at the University of California, for helpful reviews of the manuscript. I am also indebted to Richard S. Westfall, Professor of the History of Science at Indiana University, and to Ann Palfreyman of Palomar Observatory for generous help with illustrations.

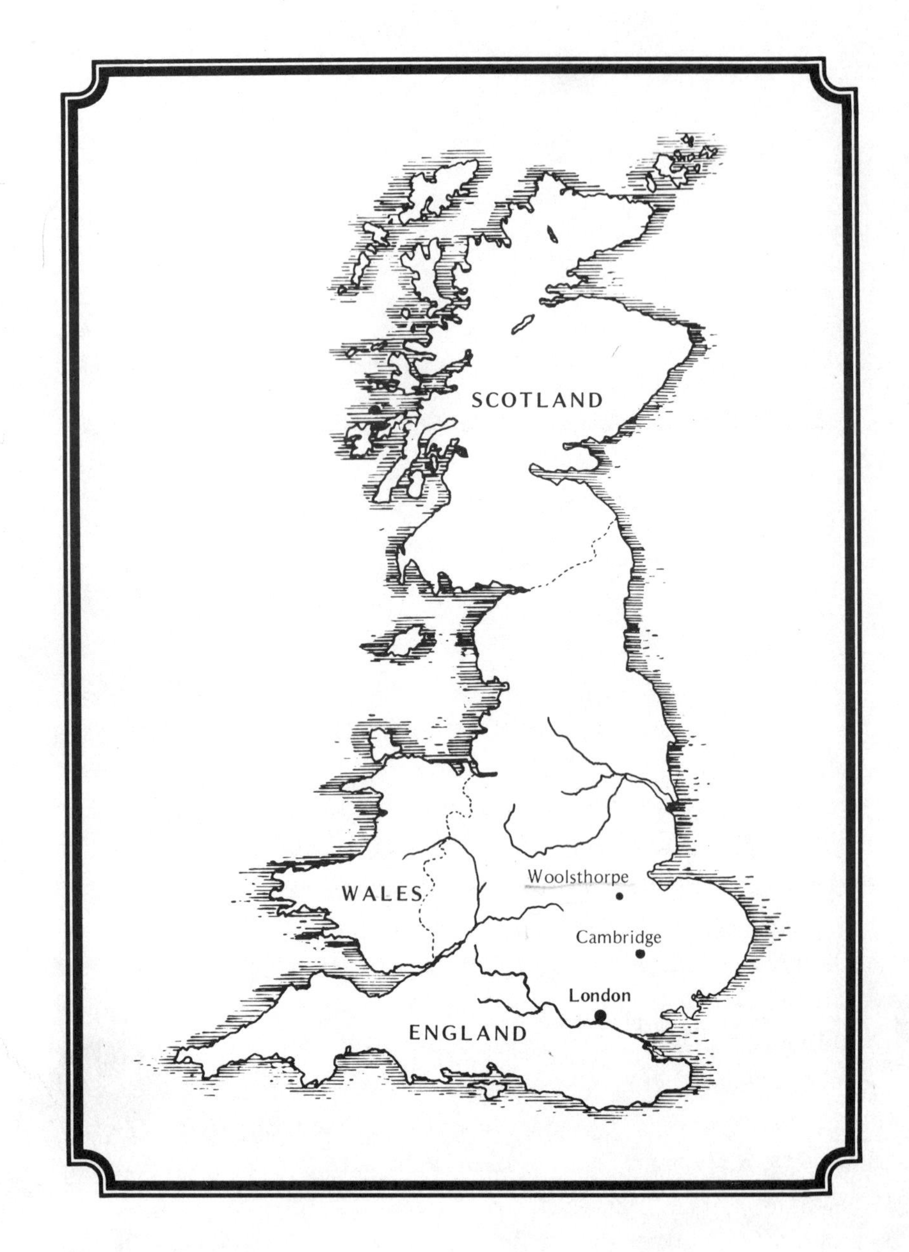

Newton's England.

1

Farmer's Son

Many people feel he lived to become the greatest scientist ever. But those who saw him on Christmas Day in 1642, when he first drew a breath, wondered whether he would live at all. Born long before he was due, he would easily have fit into a quart mug, according to his mother. And he was so frail that he was not expected to survive the day.

The newborn Isaac Newton was named after his father, a young man who owned a modest farm in the small Lincolnshire community of Woolsthorpe, about a hundred miles north of London. Isaac the father never saw Isaac the son, for he died several months before his son's birth.

Hannah Newton, Isaac's mother, may not have rejected her fatherless child, but she didn't hesitate to leave him when he was still very young. When Isaac was two, she remarried and put her son, and the farm as well, in the care of her mother. Although Hannah lived little more than a mile away and so could have seen her son often, she was well occupied with rearing the three children of her new marriage.

Knowledge of Isaac Newton's early life is sketchy. He went to nearby schools to learn the basics and must have done well enough. At age 11 he was entered in the King's School in Grantham, a school where one could prepare for the university. That mostly meant studying a great deal of Latin. Grantham, the market town for Woolsthorpe, was about seven miles away.

Young Newton began poorly at the King's School. In fact, he was rated next to the bottom of the class. But then something happened to change that dramatically. The boy just above him in class standing kicked him in the stomach as they were going to school one morning. Newton reacted by challenging the boy to a fight after school and beating him. Still annoyed, he decided to beat him in schoolwork as well. Once he began working on his new challenge, Newton's ability quickly carried him to the top of the class.

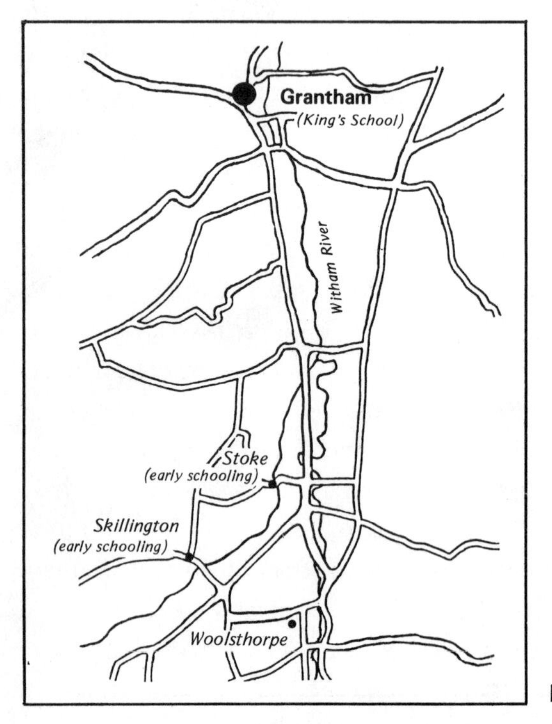

Newton's home country.

Newton's home in Woolsthorpe (as it appeared in 1946).

Besides his ability in his studies, Newton had an early knack for building gadgets of all sorts—kites, lanterns, water clocks, sundials, model waterwheels. He once watched a windmill being constructed in Grantham and made a working model of it. He even designed the model so that when the wind failed to blow, he could insert a mouse in the works and run it by mouse power.

His kite flying also took an inventive turn. Not content with the ordinary joys of kite flying, he devised a lantern that could be carried aloft by his kite. Flown in the dark of night, the airborne lantern was reported to be a terrifying sight to the people of those times, who weren't used to seeing moving lights in the sky.

While in school in Grantham, Newton lived with friends of his mother named Clark. Mr. Clark was a druggist in town and seems to have welcomed the help of his young boarder in mixing his potions. Probably from preparing drugs in those early days, Newton developed an interest in chemistry that continued through his life.

The King's School at Grantham.

Newton's studies at the King's School were interrupted after four years. His mother, who had returned to the Woolsthorpe farm after her husband's death a few years before, decided that her eldest boy was needed to help run the farm. Good with his hands as well as his brain, she could have expected him to be great at the job.

But young Newton didn't take well to his new occupation. If he was supposed to be watching the sheep or the cows, his nose was likely to be in a book as the animals roamed free. Or he might be busy making a model of a waterwheel to try in a nearby stream. The chores of farming interested him not at all.

Newton's destiny was often hinted at by his behavior during that period. One day journeying home from Grantham, Newton dismounted to ease the burden on his horse in going up a particularly steep hill. Deep in thought, he forgot to remount at the crest of the hill and arrived home after having trudged miles on foot leading the horse by its bridle. The absentminded scholar was being born.

His mother took two years to be convinced that her first child wasn't cut out to be a farmer. Helping to convince her were two men who saw hints of genius in her son—the headmaster of the King's School and her brother. The headmaster, who had come to recognize the brilliance of the young student, was so anxious that Newton continue his education that he offered not to charge the usual fees if he returned to the school. And her brother, after finding Newton under a hedge working on mathematics when he should have been doing farm chores, suggested that his studious nephew should attend Cambridge University, where he himself had gone.

Accepting their advice, his mother sent Isaac back to the King's School in Grantham with the aim of preparing for Cambridge. Her quart-mug son, she was forced to admit, had developed a mind that would never be content unless it was filled with more than a farmer's life could provide.

2

Cambridge Scholar

Newton's second stay in Grantham was short. After just one more school year at the King's School, he was admitted to Cambridge as a "subsizar"—a student who would earn his way in part by being a servant to better-heeled students. The year was 1661. Newton was 18.

Although Newton was unusual in many ways, he seems to have been quite usual in one way—he left behind a sweetheart. He had become a good friend of his landlady's daughter, Anne Storey. According to her testimony years later (Newton never mentioned it), the two had decided they would be married after Newton completed his schooling.

Not much is known about his years of study at Cambridge. Evidence that he was a serious student comes from one story that survives. Early in his university days he roomed with a student who often gave parties in their quarters, which apparently were not enjoyed by Newton. Wandering about the university grounds one evening to get away from the din, Newton came upon another student who was doing much the same. He too had a party-loving roommate. The solution was obvious. Newton's noisy roommate and his newfound friend traded places, and everyone was happier.

Stories from those days tell of early flashes of genius displayed by the young Newton. Invited to attend lectures on the book *Optics*, written by the German astronomer Johannes Kepler, Newton studied the book ahead of time and began the course with a better understanding than the lecturer.

Newton's interest in experimenting also showed itself during his college years. One experiment nearly damaged his eyes permanently. Trying to observe some strange colors he had heard about, he looked too long at the sun. For days afterward he found he could see the image of the sun that had been burned into his retina. Only by spending several days in darkness did he recover his normal vision.

His normal vision, though, was normal only to bookish types. He was nearsighted. Though his interest in optics continued, he never wore glasses. With no need in those days for sharp eyesight on the highway, good distance vision was hardly a necessity—especially in one who had no interest in sports. In later years he used his poor eyes as an excuse for not making astronomical observations.

His color vision may also have been defective. At least, in the many color experiments he would later make, he often called on an assistant to judge the colors.

Newton earned his degree in three and a half years. And so, early in 1665 he might have sped north to claim the fiancee he had left in Grantham and then settled into the life of a happily married—and now well-educated—country gentlemen. But it didn't happen that way. Newton had no notion of quitting his studies so soon. He had come to enjoy the academic life.

Anne Storey soon realized that there was little room in Newton's life for her. Although she married not long after, she

The river Cam as it passes Trinity College, Newton's home at Cambridge.

and Newton remained close friends. As far as anyone knows, the breakup of their romance ended for Newton what little he had of a love life.

Shortly after he earned his degree, Newton's idea of staying on at Cambridge was upset, though only temporarily. The Great Plague, which began in London late in 1664, threatened Cambridge as the summer of 1665 came on. The university was quickly closed and Newton retreated to the less-populated Woolsthorpe, where he spent almost two years as the plague ran its course.

For Newton the forced stay in his old home was a remarkably productive time. Some writers have called them "the miraculous years." By his account, at least, he came up with all three of the big ideas that would make him famous. The first idea was the origin of color. The second was the nature of gravity. The third was the mathematical method now known as calculus. Any one of those ideas would have been enough to put Newton's name in the history books. That he should have had all three during the short space of his Woolsthorpe "vacation" while in his early twenties still astounds scientists.

Back in Cambridge after the plague had ended—quelled some felt, by the Great Fire of London in 1666—Newton made rapid progress. He soon had a fellowship and not long after that a master's degree. Then in 1669, when he was still 26, he became professor of mathematics.

The position that Newton was chosen to fill had been created six years before through the generosity of a man named Lucas. The first to become Lucasian Professor of Mathematics, as the position was called, was Isaac Barrow, who guided Newton's mathematical studies during his student days. When Barrow became aware of the brilliance of his student, he took almost the first opportunity to resign so that Newton could fill his shoes. For Barrow himself it was no great sacrifice, as he was anxious to turn his own attention to the study of religion. But for Newton, of course, it was a great honor.

Newton's duties as Lucasian Professor were light. He was expected to hold conferences twice a week with students. And once a week during the fall term he gave a lecture. By all reports Newton wasn't exactly a spellbinder in the lecture room. Often he would show up for the lecture and find no one waiting to listen.

Newton was not impressive physically. He was of average height or less and not considered good-looking. Like the traditional professor with his mind on more important matters, he was inclined to be untidy in his dress. But if Newton failed to cut a figure in the classroom, he soon made a name for himself as a scientist.

Isaac Barrow.

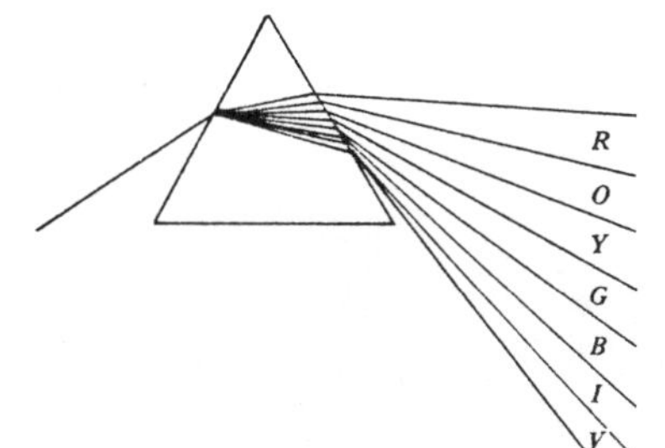

3

The Key to Color

Just how Newton got his hands on a prism isn't known for sure. But it was a happy event for science, for it inspired a series of investigations that answered many questions about color.

An obvious fact about a prism is that it does things to any ray of light that passes through it. To start with, the ray is bent by the prism. But the prism may also affect the color. In particular, the white light of the sun may become colored as it passes through a prism.

Trying to explain the color, scientists of Newton's time decided that a prism in some way changes the character of the sunlight. Some described the effect as a "darkening" of the brilliant light of the sun. A little darkening changed the white of the sun to red or orange or yellow—the "bright colors." More changed it to the "dark colors"—green or blue or violet.

But Newton thought he had a better idea. The prism, Newton decided, didn't actually change the character of the sunlight. It simply revealed it. Sunlight, he guessed, was a mixture of different colors that were each bent differently by a prism. In passing through a prism each color veered off in a different direction and so could be seen.

To test his idea Newton first cut a small hole in the shade covering the window of his room. That made the darkened room into a sort of pinhole camera. As a result, when the sun was low enough, its rays passing through the hole projected a two-inch image of the sun on the opposite wall some 20 or so feet away.

Newton then put a prism in the way of the beam so that it bent the beam upward. If all the light passing through had been bent the same amount, that would simply have moved the image of the sun higher on the wall. But it also spread out the image. Where before it was only about two inches from top to bottom, it was now over ten inches. And as expected, the color changed too. Instead of being white from top to bottom, it was violet at the top and red at the bottom, with a range of colors between.

Although Newton's experiment seemed to support his idea about the nature of sunlight, he recognized that it was hardly an ironclad proof. In his experiment the violet end of the image on the wall came from light that had passed through a greater thickness of glass than the red end. By the common view, it would not be surprising that it was more "darkened."

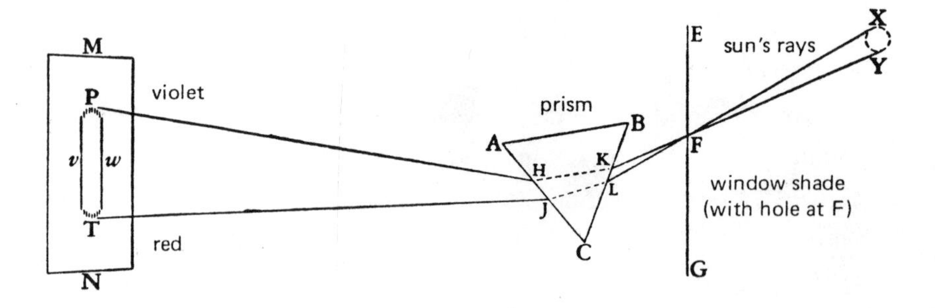

Newton's diagram of his experiment that spread out the sun's image. (Some labels added.)

To answer such an argument, Newton made further tests on the colored light he had gotten from the sun's rays. If the common view was right, it should be possible to change the red light in the image to orange or yellow or any "darker" color. But when Newton passed it through a second prism, the red light stayed red. Even passing it through a blue piece of glass or reflecting it from a green piece of paper did not change it from its original red color (though often much of the light was lost).

Newton called the colorful image he got by passing the sun's rays through a prism a "spectrum," the word still used for it. Although the spectrum had no natural divisions, each color blending into the next, Newton decided he could identify—with the help of an assistant—seven basic colors: red, orange, yellow, green, blue, indigo, and violet. Today nobody thinks of indigo as being a separate color. But Newton liked the idea of having seven colors to match the seven notes of the musical scale.

A thorough experimenter, Newton went on to discover what happened when the various colors of the spectrum were mixed. Mixing all of them together gave white again, as expected. But so did mixing selected colors. Red and blue-green light, when shining on the same spot, looked much like pale sunlight—"some faint anonymous color," suggested Newton. Orange and blue, or yellow and violet, gave the same result. Such colors that look white when mixed are now called "complementary."

Newton also discovered that not all colors are displayed in the spectrum. Mixing colors closer together than complementary colors, he found, did give spectral colors. Red and yellow light, for example, gave orange—also a color of the spectrum. But mixing colors farther apart than complementary colors gave nonspectral colors. Red and violet, for example, gave a color found nowhere among the colors of the spectrum. So did red and indigo, and orange and violet. Following Newton, scientists of today reserve the word "purple" for such a color. Unlike any other colors, the various purples always need contributions from at least two parts of the sun's spectrum.

Newton constructed a color circle to be used in deciding how colors combine. As in modern color circles, colors on opposite sides were intended to be complementary. Newton failed to give purple a clear place in his circle, only suggesting that colors "in or near" the red-violet border were purple.

In his work with light the youthful Newton showed both great skill in making experiments and great insight in interpreting them. His success at solving many of the mysteries of color earned high praise years later from Albert Einstein. "Nature to him was an open book," wrote the latter-day genius, "whose letters he could read without effort."

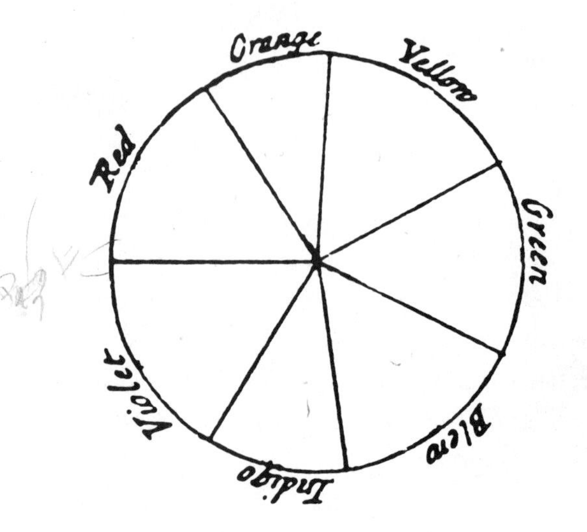

Newton's color circle.

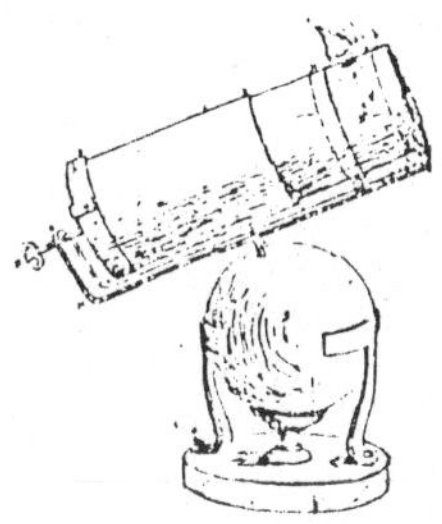

4

Fame and Frustration

Newton's discoveries about the nature of light might have gone unnoticed if he hadn't made quick use of them in devising a new telescope. It was his telescope rather than his ideas about light that brought the young scientist to the attention of the scientific community.

Newton's new understanding of light at once revealed to him a defect in ordinary telescopes. Since different colors are bent differently by a prism, they will also be focused differently by a lens. When light passes through a lens, the violet rays will come to a focus first, the red rays last. So if you try to focus a telescope on some heavenly object, you can never hope to focus it perfectly. If you focus the red rays, for example, the rays of any other color will be out of focus and will form a fuzzy image.

The obvious solution, Newton decided, was to build a telescope that focused with a mirror instead of a lens. For all colors are reflected the same by a mirror and so will come to a focus together.

Not having lost his childhood interest in making things, Newton set about making a reflecting telescope. Replacing the lens of a telescope with a mirror was not a totally new idea. A Scotsman named James Gregory had already designed a reflecting telescope. But Newton was the first to make one.

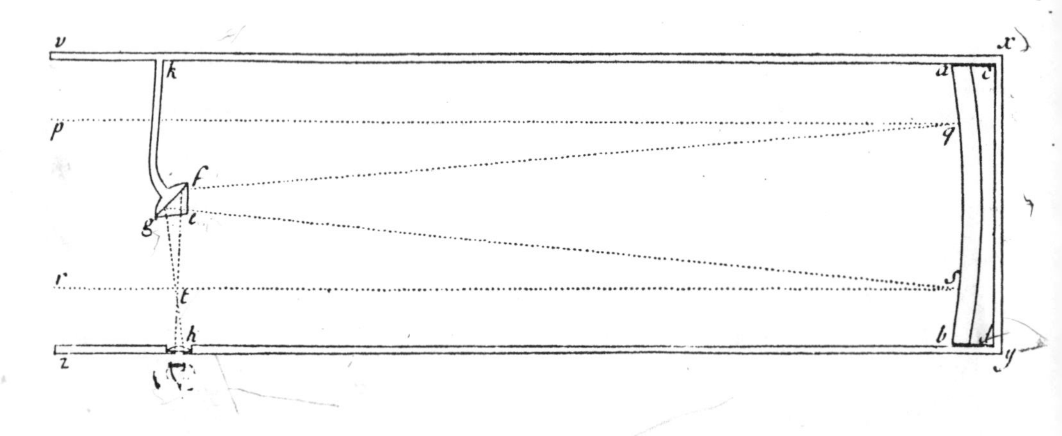

Newton's drawing of his reflecting telescope, showing how light enters from the left, reflects from the concave mirror *ab*, then from the back side *fg* of the prism to the eyepiece *h*.

Newton's creation was quite small—only six inches long with a concave mirror about an inch and a third in diameter. But with it he could see as well as with a much larger telescope that used a lens instead of a mirror.

Newton is sometimes criticized for overlooking another solution to the color problem in telescopes. Scientists since Newton have found that by using a combination of lenses made of different kinds of glass, the various colors can be focused more or less together. But Newton's solution is still the most effective and the one used in today's largest telescopes.

Although Newton wasn't quick to publicize his clever creation, news of it eventually reached the Royal Society of London, the foremost scientific society of Europe in those days. Once they learned of Newton's telescope, the members of the society asked him to send them a model. They were clearly impressed when they saw it, for they soon asked him to join the society.

Pleased that his telescope had made a hit, Newton suggested that perhaps the members would like to hear about the reason he had made it. For the idea behind the telescope, proposed Newton, was much more exciting than the instrument itself.

To his dismay, Newton found that selling his idea wasn't as easy as selling his invention. What had seemed to him so clear and certain after his painstaking experiments was not quickly accepted by his new scientific colleagues.

Part of the trouble could be blamed on Newton, for he wasn't content merely to present his discoveries. He tried also to explain them by his own theory of the nature of light. His notion was that light was made up of small particles of different sizes. The largest were the particles of red light, which were the hardest to deflect. The smallest were the particles of violet light, which were deflected much more easily. So when passed through a prism, red light bent least, violet most.

This notion didn't sit well with one member in particular, an ingenious scientist named Robert Hooke. Hooke had the position of curator of the Royal Society, which meant that he was in charge of all the equipment and exhibits of the society. He also had the challenging job of performing several experiments each week for the entertainment and enlightenment of the members who attended the weekly meetings. Like Newton, Hooke was a lifelong bachelor. But he perhaps had more excuse, for his body had become deformed during childhood. Though he was a scientist of some fame, no portrait of Hooke survives.

Hooke's view was that light was much like sound. Sound is carried by pressure waves in air. Light, Hooke proposed, was carried by similar waves in "ether," that mysterious substance that was then believed to fill all of otherwise unoccupied space.

Hooke saw nothing in Newton's experiments that ruled out his own wave picture of light. And in fact nothing did. The different colors of light could as easily be thought of as the result of different wavelengths of light as of different sizes of particles.

But besides rejecting Newton's particle theory of light, Hooke also rejected Newton's view that sunlight consisted of a whole spectrum of colors. Somehow he wasn't able to accept what Newton had proved while discarding what he hadn't.

Newton was distressed to find that he had to spend a great deal of time defending his results because of scientists such as Hooke. He seemed forever to be writing letters to scientists on both sides of the English Channel patiently explaining why their objections to his results weren't correct. He eventually became quite impatient, for all that anyone needed to do was to try his experiments and discover the truth for himself.

From these early encounters with scientific criticism, Newton developed a touchiness that stayed with him throughout his life. As he grew older, he got along beautifully with scientists who praised him. But he often became bitter toward those who challenged his ideas.

His clashes with Hooke over the nature of light continued for several years. Newton became so bitter that Hooke eventually tried to soothe his rival's feelings. He wrote him a friendly letter protesting that, like Newton, he was only seeking the truth. Verbally patting him on the head—and quite likely annoying Newton further—he praised Newton for adding to the work that Hooke had begun. Hooke regretted, he said, that their argument had been made public, and he hoped that future disputes could be held in private.

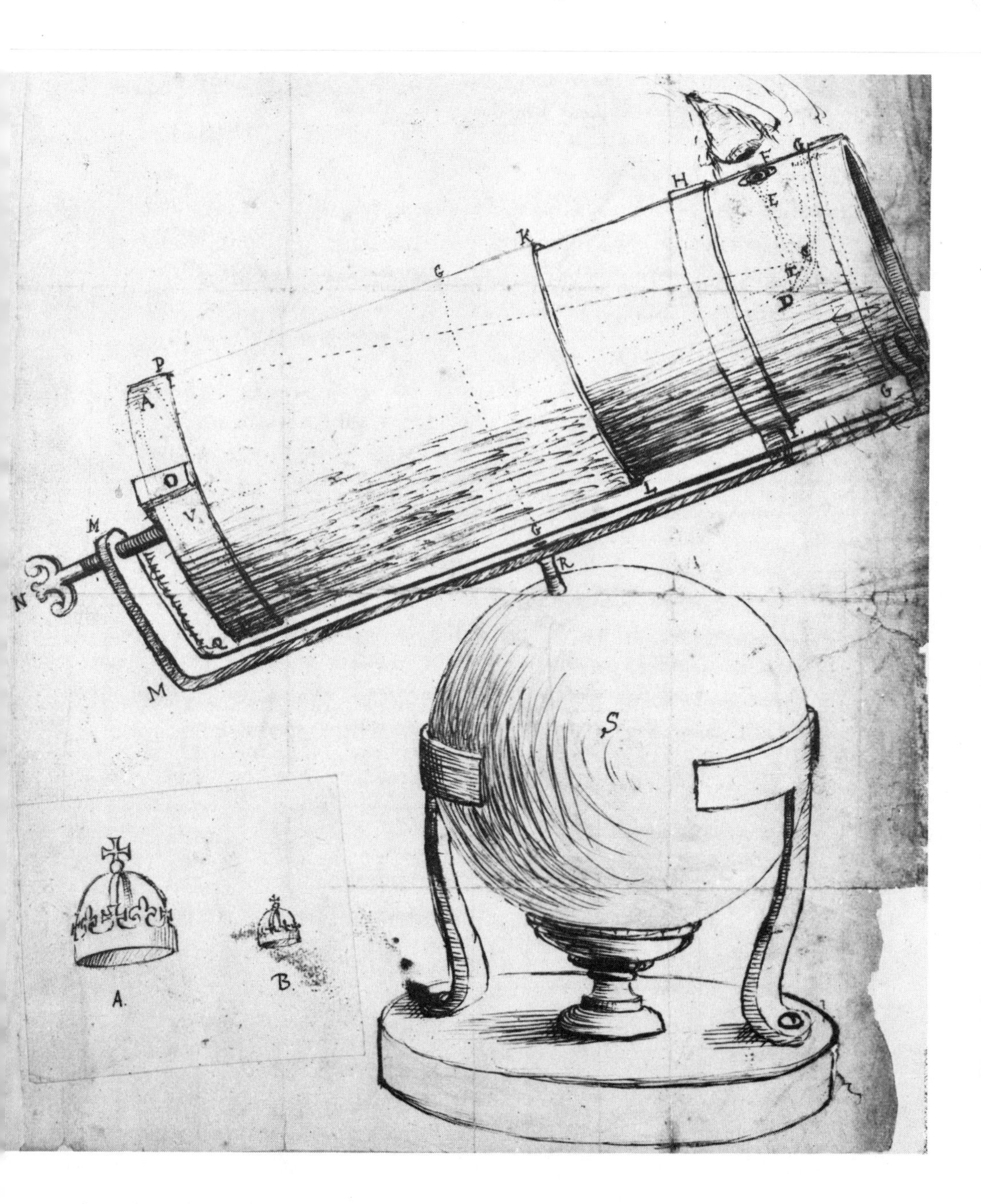

Newton's reflecting telescope. The crowns show a weathervane ornament as seen by Newton's 6-inch-long telescope (A) and an ordinary 25-inch-long telescope (B).

Newton answered with what seemed an equally friendly letter. But he made a remark that could have rubbed Hooke the wrong way. Giving credit to Hooke and to the French scientist Descartes—now dead—for their early work on light, Newton commented: "If I have seen farther, it is by standing on the shoulders of giants." The image of Newton on his shoulders seeing farther than he, one can guess, could easily have displeased the proud Hooke.

Newton's experience with trying to sell his ideas about light drove him back into his shell. He had presented his ideas to the Royal Society in 1672, when he was not yet 30, and had spent the next few years defending them. But then he retreated.

Newton was eventually convinced by his friends, many years later, that he should disclose all of his experiments and ideas on light. In 1704 he published a book called *Opticks* (spelling in those days was largely a matter of personal choice). You might imagine that Newton, then 61, would have mellowed with age—and fame—and been willing to risk the renewed criticism his book could bring. But perhaps more important was the fact that he had outlived his prime critic. Robert Hooke had died in 1703.

The Newton-Hooke dispute about the nature of light continued after Hooke's death. But the publication of *Opticks* when Newton was at the peak of his fame gave the particle theory of light a great boost. For many years after that, most scientists followed Newton's lead.

The modern view of light borrows a little from Hooke and a little from Newton. Light isn't so simple as either rival imagined. It behaves something like a wave, though not a pressure wave. And it comes in particles of a sort—photons, they're now called. But the truth is that light, like electrons or other small particles of nature, can't be fully described in familiar terms. Hooke and Newton, looking for a simple picture, were both bound to fail.

5

Ideas From an Apple

While it was a prism that started Newton wondering about color, it was an apple that started him wondering about gravity.

The story of Newton and the apple sounds like a myth. But it comes from Newton himself. One fall day in Woolsthorpe during the plague, an apple from a nearby tree fell at Newton's feet. That chance event, Newton reported later, started him thinking about gravity.

Clearly, Newton decided, the earth's gravity is something that can act at a distance. The apple was not touching the earth, yet it was drawn to the earth by a force. Was it possible that this force of gravity that reached as far as the apple also reached as far as the moon?

These passing thoughts led Newton to the idea that the gravity of the earth might explain the motion of the moon about the earth. In the same way, he decided, the gravity of the sun might explain the motion of the planets about the sun.

To test his idea, Newton figured out what force is needed to keep an object moving in a circular orbit, which is a first approximation to the orbit followed by the planets or the moon. Figuring that out was itself quite a feat. But, as Newton said later, "in those days I was in the prime of my age for invention."

His next step, Newton reported, was to use that result to find the forces that guide the planets. The speeds of the planets decrease as their distances from the sun increase, following a law discovered by Johannes Kepler, the German scientist whose work Newton had studied in college. To agree with Kepler's result, and his own, Newton found that the forces on the planets must also decrease. The law the forces must follow, he discovered, was an "inverse square law." A planet twice as far away must be guided by a force that is one quarter as large, a planet three times as far by a force one ninth as large, and so on.

Newton checked his newfound law for the moon and found it worked there too—"pretty nearly." To keep the moon in orbit, he calculated, required a gravity at the moon about one thirty-six-hundredth as great as the gravity at the earth's surface. That result followed an inverse square law, provided distances were measured from the earth's center. The earth's gravity, it seemed, behaved as if it stemmed from the very center of the earth.

It seems like an exciting discovery, but Newton kept the news to himself. Quite possibly his discovery wasn't as clear and certain as it sounds, for the story of it comes from his reminiscences in his old age. But whatever the truth, following his Woolsthorpe interlude, Newton put his ideas about gravity on the back burner for a while.

For about a dozen years, in fact, Newton seems to have had no more thoughts about gravity and motion. But then late in 1679 he got a letter that stirred his interest again. It was the friendliest of letters, but it would have an unfriendly outcome. The writer was Robert Hooke.

It was a chatty letter. Hooke told of some ideas he and others had had about motion and wondered if Newton might have any thoughts on these matters. What did he think, for

Johannes Kepler.

example, about the ideas of a French scientist who put the sun as well as the planets into orbit? Newton reacted in the same friendly vein, admitting that he really hadn't thought about such things in some time—in fact, had not even been aware of the ideas Hooke spoke of.

Newton then, almost as an afterthought, described a "fancy" of his for showing the earth's rotation on its axis. His idea was to drop an object such as a pistol bullet from a height and see where it landed. If the earth didn't rotate, the object would land on a spot directly below. But since the earth rotates from west to east, the object should land, Newton argued, a little to the east of that spot.

As Newton pointed out, that may not be exactly what you'd expect. Since the earth's surface is moving from west to east, you might expect the object to lag behind after it is dropped and land to the west. But the truth is that the object is also moving from west to east, and since it is farther from the earth's center, it is moving faster than the earth's surface.

Newton included a sketch in his letter showing how the object would descend to earth. He also showed what would happen if the object could travel below the earth's surface. He traced a curve that rather quickly reached the center of the earth, making only a slight spiral as it traveled inward.

Newton would later curse his own haste, for he made two small errors in what he wrote. First, the object would not land directly to the east. In a northern latitude such as England's, it would land to the south of its starting point as well as to the east. Then the object, if not slowed by anything, would not spiral quickly to the center of the earth. It would go into some sort of elongated orbit swinging about the earth's center.

Hooke was quick to point out these minor slips to Newton. What was worse, he did not keep it a private matter between the two, as he had promised in his earlier letter about light. He read his reply to Newton before the Royal Society.

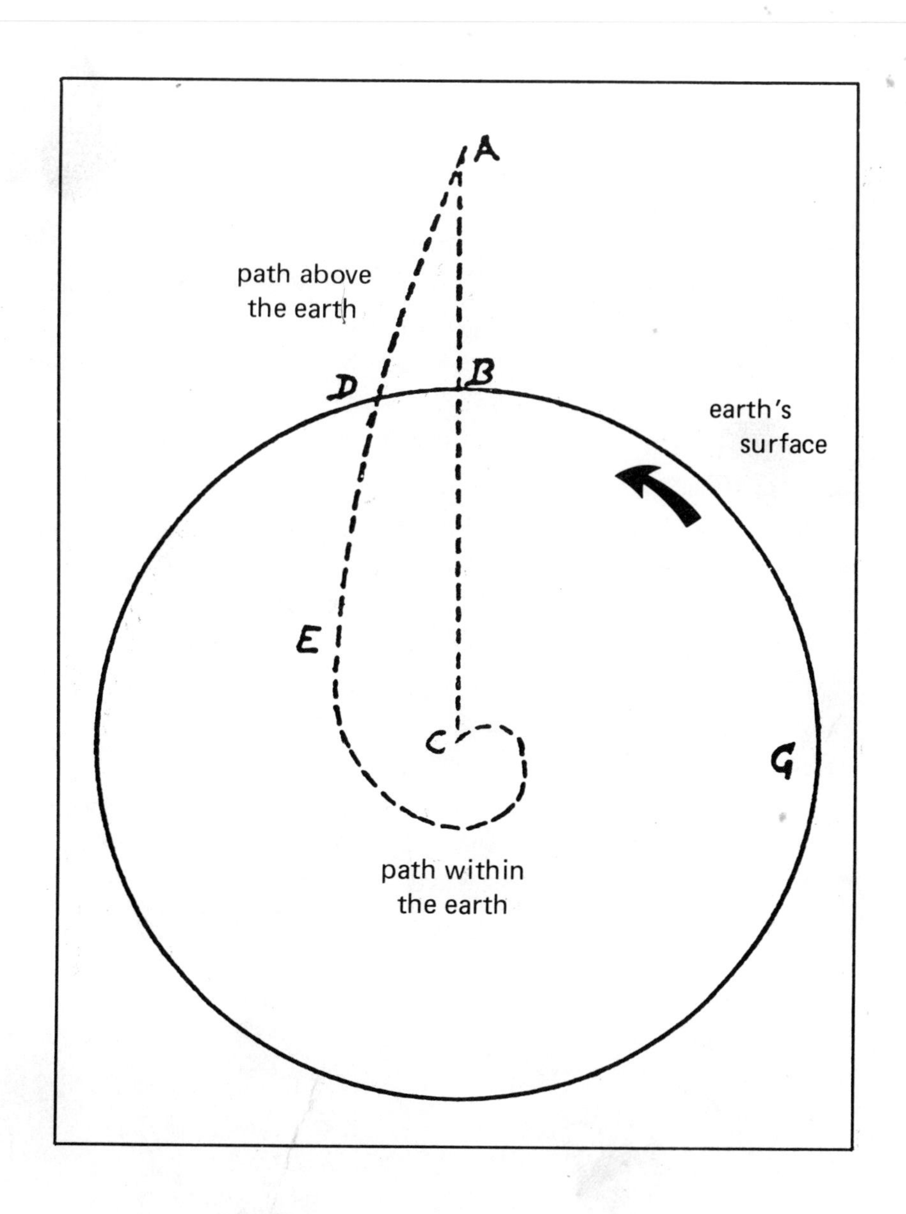

Newton's sketch of the fall of a bullet. (Some labels added.)

Newton had to admit that Hooke was right. But he hardly thanked him for his helpful criticism. The ill will that Newton had felt toward Hooke during their clashes over light was now rekindled. And this time it was not to die.

Hooke seemed unaware of the bad feelings he had caused. He performed Newton's experiment several times and did find that the object fell to the east and south of its original location above the earth. But scientists since then have been unable to explain how he succeeded so well. With the heights and methods he used, they argue, he shouldn't have been able to detect the earth's motion at all. Hooke happily reported his findings to Newton, though he did admit that they weren't terribly consistent—probably, he thought, because of drafts.

Hooke's letters to Newton were especially interesting because they suggested that gravity follows an inverse square law. How he had gotten that notion he didn't say. But it was not so difficult by then. For the conclusions that Newton had reached during the plague about the force needed to give circular motion had since been reached by the Dutch scientist Christian Huygens. And Huygens, unlike the secretive Newton, had let the world know about it.

Hooke's casual mention of the inverse square law of gravity, as it happened, would eventually create more bitterness between the two scientists.

6

Questions Over Coffee

After his embarrassment at the hands of Hooke, Newton broke off his letter writing. But evidence of a few years later suggests that he did not immediately break off his thoughts about motion and gravity.

It all started in January 1684 in a London coffeehouse where three members of the Royal Society were chatting after a weekly meeting of the society. It was a stellar cast. The senior member of the group was the famous architect Christopher Wren, 51, who had been a scientist of some note before he turned his talents to architecture. Close behind in age was Robert Hooke, 48, perpetual thorn in Newton's side. The third member of the group was a young astronomer whose chief claims to fame were yet to come, Edmond Halley, 27.

Halley began the conversation. Like Newton and Hooke, he had decided that gravity must follow an inverse square law. But that conclusion was based on circular motion, he noted, and the planets follow elliptical paths as they orbit the sun. Did an inverse square law work for elliptical as well as circular motion?

Halley, a skillful mathematician himself, had tackled that question without success. He now presented it to Hooke and Wren.

Wren could offer no help, but Hooke quickly claimed he had solved the problem. Yes, he proposed, an elliptical orbit did indeed call for an inverse square law. But when pressed for his proof, Hooke wouldn't reveal it. He wanted others to struggle with the problem first, he claimed, so they would recognize the value of his solution when he made it public.

If Hooke could play games, so could Wren. In the hope of flushing out whatever knowledge Hooke might have, Wren offered a prize of an expensive book to whichever of his friends could come up with a solution to the problem within two months.

The two months passed without a claim for Wren's prize. But Halley's interest in the problem persisted. So during the summer he journeyed to Cambridge to present the problem to Newton.

Newton quickly assured Halley that he had solved the problem some years before. But it began to look as if he might be as much a gamester as Hooke. When he tried to put his hands on the solution, he couldn't find it. Newton promised that he would work it out again, though, and send it to Halley in London.

Once he got working on the problem, Newton apparently became intrigued, for he went well beyond merely re-solving the original problem. He developed a series of lectures for his fall classes, all dealing with problems about motion.

In November, more than fulfilling his promise, Newton sent Halley the notes for all the lectures. It was a fateful step. When Halley saw them, he was so excited that he journeyed back to Cambridge to convince Newton to publish his ideas. And somehow the youthful Halley overcame Newton's reluctance to expose himself again to possible criticism. Newton agreed to publish.

Just what Newton first intended to publish, no one knows—perhaps little more than his lecture notes. But once he started to work on his ideas, he seemed to become infected with an

Edmond Halley.

urge to explore them further. He solved problem after problem about motion—not only the motion of planets through space but also the motion of more ordinary objects through more ordinary surroundings.

He put his work together in three parts, which he called "books." The first book dealt with the motion of objects in space (or at least with little fluid resistance). The second dealt with the motion of objects through fluids. The third contained applications of his results from the first two books.

Newton must have sensed that he was creating a masterpiece, for he spared no effort. He often worked well into the night, getting along with little sleep. And often he forgot to eat. Supper from the night before might sit unnoticed, then serve as breakfast the next morning.

Book I was ready for publication in the spring of 1686. Newton sent the manuscript to the Royal Society, which agreed to publish it. Halley would serve as editor. With his biggest fan guiding the publication, it looked as if Newton's work would have smooth sailing. But as it turned out, the sailing was far from smooth.

The first problem was Robert Hooke. After he saw the manuscript, Hooke protested that Newton should give him credit for suggesting an inverse square law for gravity. Newton was furious, for he had developed the idea himself without help from Hooke. But Hooke, of course, pointed to the letters he had written to Newton disclosing the law.

Grudgingly, Newton agreed to include a statement giving Hooke some credit. But what little credit Newton gave him Hooke had to share. The inverse square law, Newton suggested, had been noted by Wren, Hooke, and Halley—the coffeehouse trio.

The second problem was financial. Having recently published a poorly selling book about fish, the Royal Society had insufficient funds to pay for the printing of another book. Fortunately, other funds were soon found. Halley was so eager to see the work published that he offered to finance the publication himself. So on July 5, 1686, Newton's work was given the official go-ahead by the president of the Royal Society, Samuel Pepys, a man better known today for the private life revealed by his diary than for his public life.

But the sailing still was not smooth, thanks now to Newton. Mostly as a result of his trouble with Hooke, Newton decided that he would withhold publication of Book III. That part of the work, he feared, could provide a field day for his critics. With some difficulty Halley talked Newton out of his decision. To many of the readers, argued Halley, that would be the most useful part of the work—perhaps the only part they could understand!

Newton put the finishing touches on his great work early in the spring of 1687. Printing was completed that summer. Anyone who has become familiar with the total work has always been amazed by how much Newton accomplished in so short a time. The author, as his masterpiece hit the bookshops, was 44.

As in any work designed for scientists abroad as well as at home, Newton wrote in Latin. Its title was *Philosophiae Naturalis Principia Mathematica*, which can be translated as *Mathematical Principles of Natural Philosophy*. It is now usually called simply the *Principia*.

The importance of the book was immediately recognized. So was its difficulty. A story goes that a student on the Cambridge campus pointed out Newton to a friend as the man who had written a book so difficult that he couldn't understand it himself. Though it was a difficult book, the *Principia* was also a remarkably influential one. It was revised twice during Newton's lifetime and translated into English soon after his death.

The publication of the *Principia* at once set Newton apart from ordinary humans. In an ode to Newton included in the first edition, Halley expressed a sentiment that would often be repeated: "Nearer the gods no mortal may approach."

PHILOSOPHIÆ NATURALIS PRINCIPIA MATHEMATICA.

Autore *J S. NEWTON*, *Trin. Coll. Cantab. Soc.* Matheſeos Profeſſore *Lucaſiano*, & Societatis Regalis Sodali.

IMPRIMATUR.
S. PEPYS, *Reg. Soc.* PRÆSES.
Julii 5. 1686.

LONDINI,

Juſſu *Societatis Regiæ* ac Typis *Joſephi Streater*. Proſtat apud plures Bibliopolas. *Anno* MDCLXXXVII.

Title page of the *Principia*.

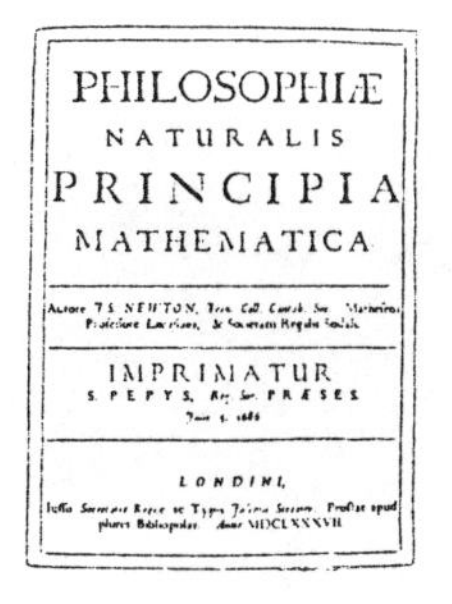
PHILOSOPHIÆ
NATURALIS
PRINCIPIA
MATHEMATICA

IMPRIMATUR

LONDINI,

7

The *Principia*

The most impressive contribution of the *Principia* was its collection of solutions. Newton seemed to have solved every pressing problem of motion both in the heavens and on the earth. But more important, at least in the long run, was its collection of laws for solving those problems. Newton distilled his understanding of the dynamics of movement into three laws of motion and a law of gravitation.

The laws of motion were presented in a short section that preceded Book I of the *Principia*. They were, Newton generously suggested, nothing new. But nobody had stated them before. Today they are unquestionably "Newton's" laws of motion.

The first law was by itself no great help. It said that anything that is moving will keep moving at the same speed and in the same direction unless some force acts to change that. Newton credited the law to Galileo, the famous Italian scientist who died the year Newton was born. But the truth is that Galileo believed only that the speed would not change. In his mind, the moon circling the earth needed no force to keep it on its curving path.

Newton two years after publication of the *Principia*. (First surviving portrait.)

Newton's second law was more significant. It introduced the idea of momentum, which is simply the mass of an object times its velocity. According to the second law, a force acting on any object changes its momentum by a corresponding amount—either in size or in direction or both. Newton also credited this law to Galileo, who undoubtedly deserved even less credit here.

Although it certainly did not then, by now Newton's third law has a familiar ring even to the nonscientist: For every action there is an equal and opposite reaction. "If you press a stone with your finger," pointed out Newton, "the finger is also pressed by the stone." For this law he gave credit to three of his fellow scientists: the scientist-turned-architect Christopher Wren, the Dutch scientist Christian Huygens, and John Wallis, who was then professor of mathematics at Oxford. The three had each found they could explain the behavior of colliding balls by assuming that the opposing forces on the balls during the collision were the same size. It is safe to say that none of them dreamed of the uses that Newton would have for the law.

The three laws of motion are really three faces of a single idea, which is expressed in its fullest form by the second law. The first law is easily seen to be an outcome of the second. And Newton himself showed how the third law can be proved by the second. But whether one law or three, Newton provided in this brief introduction the basic tools needed to solve all problems of motion.

Newton's other famous law, the law of gravity, was disclosed in Book I. Newton showed, of course, that the sun's gravity must follow an inverse square law in order to explain the motion of the planets. But there was more to the law than that. If the sun exerted forces on the planets, the planets must exert forces on the sun. For according to the third law, each action must have its reaction.

This thinking led quickly to the notion that gravity is universal. Every object that experiences gravity must also exert it. The apple that is pulled by the earth must itself be pulling on the earth—and pulling just as hard. The idea of universal gravitation appears to have come to Newton as he struggled with the *Principia*. The Woolsthorpe apple had started Newton thinking about gravity, but his full understanding had come much later.

Newton used his new insight into gravity to solve a problem that had troubled him since the plague years: the nature of the earth's gravity close to the earth's surface. He was able to show that the gravity of any ball-shaped object—which is nearly the shape of the earth—acts as if all the mass were at the center of the object. Whether an object is at the earth's surface (hanging on an apple tree, perhaps) or at the distance of the moon, the size of the force of gravity on the object depends on the distance from the earth's center. So his calculation in Woolsthorpe made sense.

But he showed also that this rule doesn't apply inside the ball. There the forces of gravity from the outer parts of the ball cancel one another. All that is left is the gravity from the ball of matter that is nearer the center. So if you could travel to the center of the earth, you would discover that the force of gravity dropped off steadily as you went below the surface, reaching zero at the center.

That result made Hooke's claim of discovering the law of gravity look exceedingly weak. For Hooke had suggested that gravity continues to increase as you venture beneath the earth's surface. Hooke's view of gravity, though partly correct, was no match for Newton's.

As the full title indicated, the *Principia* was full of mathematics. But Newton also made good use of experiments. That was especially true in Book II, where Newton dealt with motion through fluids. The most dramatic experiment (included in a later edition) was one in which two glass globes, one full of air and one full of mercury, were dropped 220 feet from high in the dome of St. Paul's Cathedral as a test of air resistance.

The dome of St. Paul's, the great cathedral designed by Christopher Wren, where some of Newton's experiments were performed.

Book II's most interesting result historically was Newton's calculation of the speed of sound. Newton checked his result by timing the echo from the end of a long colonnade on campus and found good agreement between what he measured and what he had calculated. Later work showed that he had measured too small a speed—an easy error to explain. But it took over a century to explain why he had also calculated too small a speed. The Frenchman who discovered his error (an incorrect way of figuring the elasticity of air) still praised Newton's result. "His theory, though imperfect," wrote the scientist, "is a monument to his genius."

Book III of the *Principia* Newton called "The System of the World." In it he showed how his ideas could be used to answer many of the questions about motion that had puzzled scientists.

Trinity College, Cambridge, showing the colonnade where Newton measured the speed of sound.

Measurements made by astronomer Cassini in France seemed to show that the earth was shaped like an American football. Newton showed that the laws of motion and gravity must give it quite a different shape. With a surface mostly of water, the spinning earth must be flattened at the poles and bulging at the equator.

In spite of the *Principia*, the Cassini view of an elongated earth didn't die at once. In France it died only fifty years later, when a French scientist traveled to Lapland and made measurements that confirmed Newton's view. The efforts of the French scientist inspired a sarcastic salute from his countryman Voltaire: "Flattener of the earth and Cassini, you have discovered in far-flung places and by tedious means what Newton discovered at home."

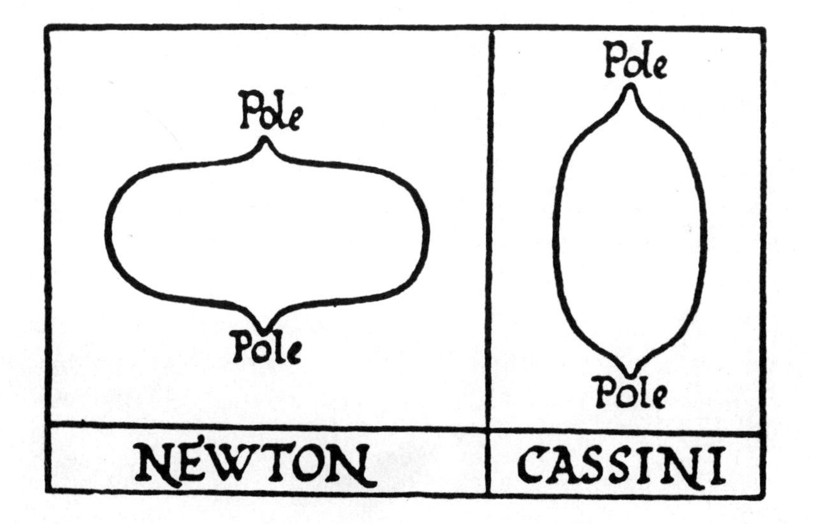

An old cartoon contrasting Newton's and Cassini's views of the earth.

Newton also discussed the tides. He showed that the seas should bulge both on the side of the earth that faces the moon and on the opposite side. Pointing out that the sun produces smaller bulges, he showed how the effect of these two great "luminaries" in our sky may add or subtract to give higher or lower tides.

Newton discovered that the earth's actual tides were well behind schedule. Instead of following beneath the moon, high tide arrived about three hours later. He explained that by the inertia of the water, but it turns out he was wrong. Later scientists have shown the cause to be friction.

If he was occasionally wrong, he was much more often right. One notable success was his explanation of the precession of the equinoxes, discovered eighteen centuries before by the Greek scientist Hipparchus.

The precession of the equinoxes is the change in the sun's apparent location in the sky on the first day of spring or fall, when the sun lies directly over the equator. To Hipparchus the sun at the start of spring appeared near the constellation Aries. But by Newton's time it had migrated to the vicinity of Pisces. This change in the spring scene, as well as a similar change in the fall, comes about because of a change in the direction of the earth's axis. The north pole of the earth, pointing now to the North Star, traces a circle in the sky over the course of 26,000 years—behaving much like the pole of a gyroscope. And during that time the equinoxes move through all the constellations of the zodiac.

Newton found the explanation for this motion of the gyroscope we call earth in the pull of the moon and the sun on the earth's bulging midsection. His calculation of about 50 seconds of precession a year came very close to the measured value.

Newton ended Book III (and the *Principia*) with a discussion of comets. Calculations he had been able to make showed that

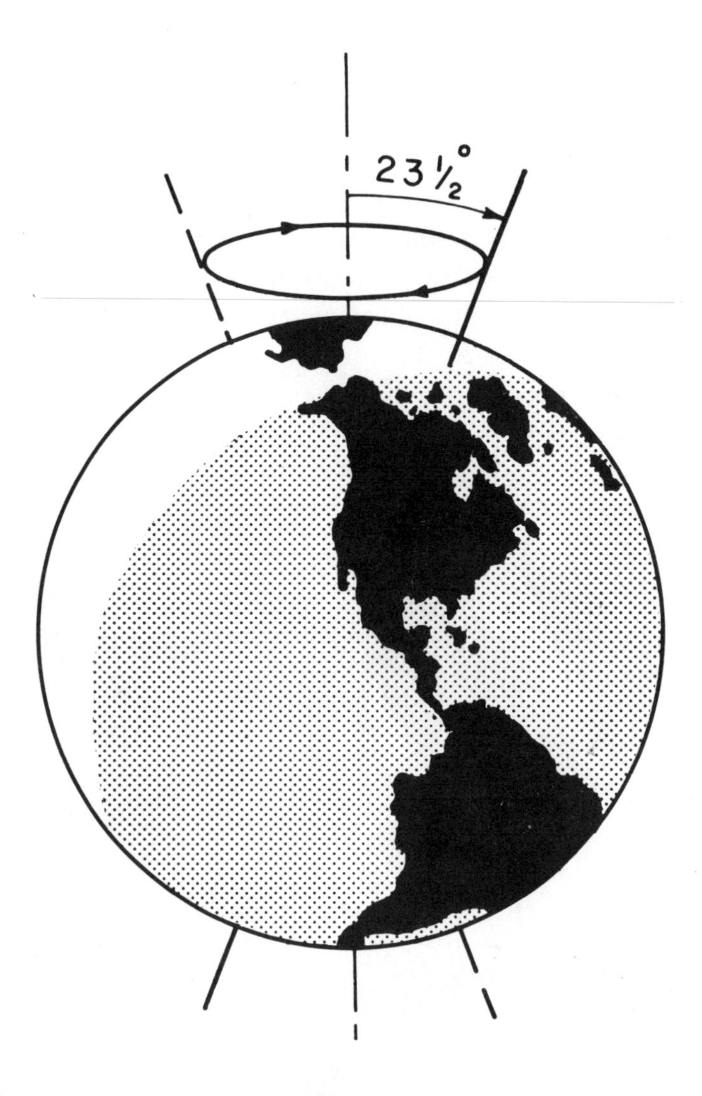

Newton showed why the earth's axis, now pointing toward the North Star, gradually changes direction over the centuries.

comets probably traveled along elliptical orbits, just as planets did. But there was one problem with comets that made that hard to prove. Any comet that had been measured was seen only along a very short part of its path. For the comet swept in from far out in space and could be seen only during the short time when it was near the sun. With so brief an encounter, it was hard to be sure whether the comet was visiting the region near the sun once and for all or would be back again another day.

That topic was a fitting end to the *Principia*, for the next step in solving the motions of the heavens was built on Newton's ideas about comets.

8

Newton's Comet

We call it Halley's comet today, not Newton's. And perhaps Newton's younger colleague deserves the credit. But without Newton and the *Principia*, Halley would never have made his discovery.

For years comets had been a matter for much speculation. Early thinking about the universe put them in the earth's atmosphere, for there seemed to be no room for them among the planets. Their paths would interfere too much with the spheres or swirls that were imagined to carry the planets on their nearly circular paths about the sun.

But Tycho Brahe, the Danish scientist known for his accurate measurements of the heavens, made measurements on a comet that showed it must lie beyond the moon. And so science had to find a place for comets among the planets, even though they traveled along much different paths.

Arguments still persisted as to just what those paths were. Some argued straight lines, some circles. There was little agreement. Even Newton, before he began the *Principia*, was confused.

In 1680 a comet disappeared behind the sun and later reappeared going in a different direction. Scientists who watched the comet argued about whether it was one comet or two. And Newton, for some years, held the second opinion.

In the *Principia* Newton showed that the visible path of a comet is like one end of a long and slender ellipse looping around the sun. He also showed how to use a few measurements of its path to decide how the end of the ellipse is positioned in the heavens. Using these ideas, he found that the comet of 1680 did loop behind the sun and reappear. No new comet was needed to explain the second appearance.

Reversing direction as the comet looped around the sun was one thing. But did it also reverse direction at the other end of its travel? That end, if it existed at all, was in some remote region of the solar system, perhaps beyond the most distant planets, where there was no hope of seeing it.

Newton's laws gave no help with the answer. According to the equations, the comet didn't have to follow the closed curve of an ellipse. It could just as easily follow the open curve of a hyperbola. The laws of gravity and motion permitted either shape.

Of course, if you see enough of the path, an ellipse can be distinguished from a hyperbola. And Newton saw enough of the path of the comet of 1680 to believe that it was an ellipse. In fact, he estimated that the orbit of that comet reached 10 to 12 times as far from the sun as the orbit of Saturn. If so, the comet would return in about 400 years.

Newton's conclusion, though, was highly tentative, and he happily accepted an offer from Edmond Halley to make an independent check. If the comet was due to return in 400 years, it must have made a visit 400 years ago. Halley proposed to search the records for a thirteenth-century comet that had followed the same path in the heavens.

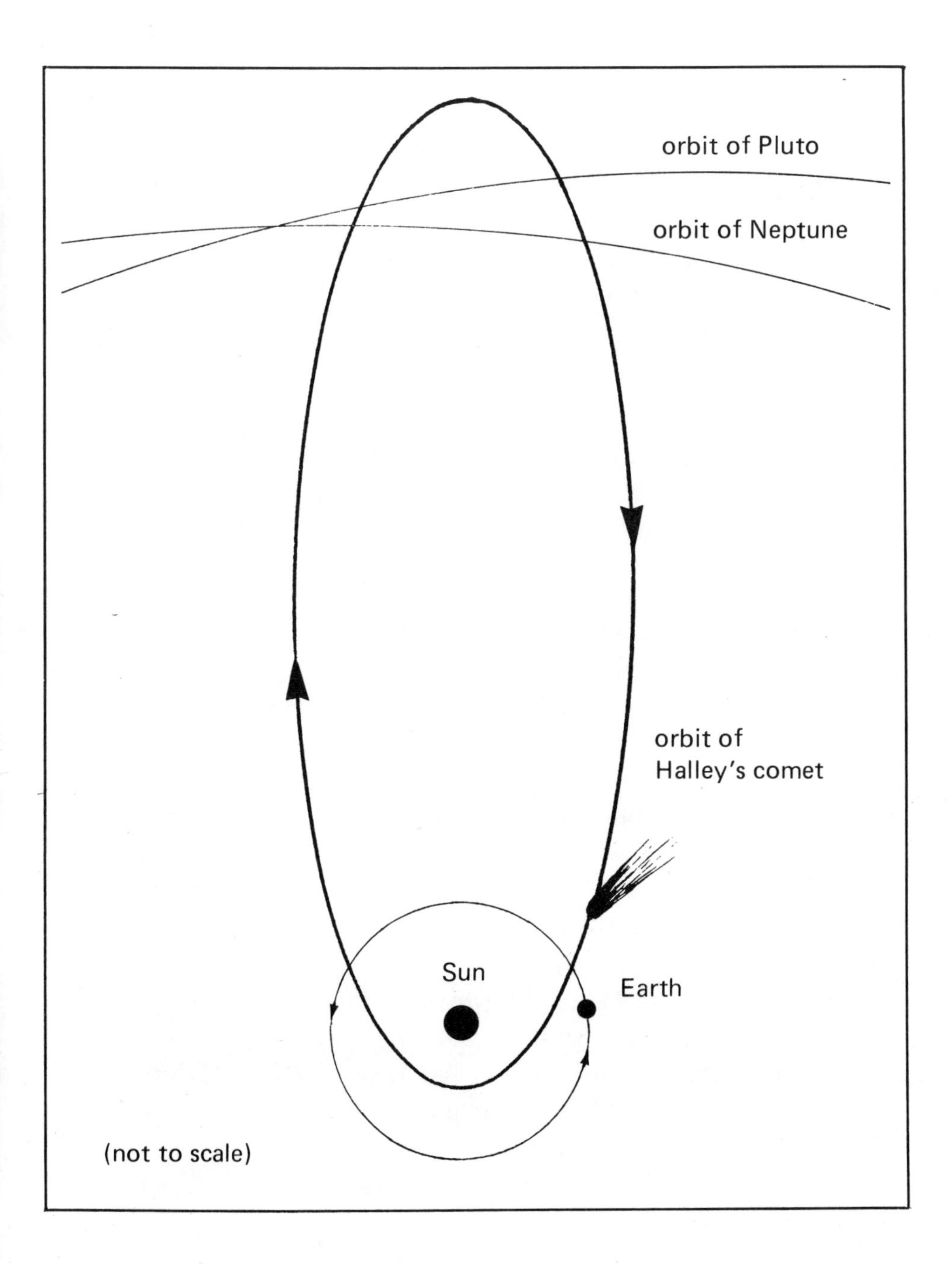

The orbit of Halley's comet, which takes it from the nearest parts of the solar system to the farthest.

Halley's search turned up no thirteenth-century comet to match the comet of 1680. But it did uncover a slower comet that traveled the same path. The comet of 1680, Halley decided, had been around at least three times before. The first record was in 44 B.C., a few months after Julius Caesar's assassination; the second in 531; and the third in 1106. These dates lie about 575 years apart. So the next visit, Halley reckoned, should come in the year 2255.

If that had been the only such comet he found, we would still be waiting to name Halley's comet. But fortunately for his fame, he found records of another comet that appeared to have come back—and that one was on a much quicker schedule. The comet of 1682, Halley discovered, was nicely matched by a comet in 1607. It was also matched by comets in 1531 and 1456. The time between visits wasn't exactly the same. But passing near a large planet, Halley decided, could change the course a little. So every 75 or 76 years, this speedy comet could be expected to reappear in the sky. With some confidence Halley predicted that it should make its next appearance in 1758 or thereabouts.

Although Halley lived to be 85, he was about 16 years short of seeing its return. But on Christmas Day 1758 a comet made its appearance in the sky. It was a little behind Halley's schedule, not reaching the vicinity of the sun until early in 1759. But it was Halley's comet of 1682 without a doubt. And it has been known as Halley's comet since.

Later astronomers have looked back further into history than Halley did and have found a long succession of visits from the same comet. The earliest record they discovered was in 240 B.C., during the lifetime of Archimedes. In 163 B.C., when the great astronomer Hipparchus probably was a child, it should also have made an appearance, but no mention of it by him or anyone else has survived. Its next appearance, though, and every other since has been established.

Halley's comet as photographed May 12, 1910.

The comet has occasionally been prominent in history. Much notice was made of it in 1066, when its visit came at the time of the Norman conquest of England. Considered a bad omen by the English, it certainly proved so for King Harold, who was killed in the Battle of Hastings during the time when the comet was visible in the English sky.

In its most recent visits the comet has had the distinction of marking the birth and death of Mark Twain, in 1835 and 1910. During the latter visit the earth passed through the comet's tail, an event feared by many—including a few scientists. But one scientist predicted that the encounter would be as spectacular as a rhinoceros in full charge colliding with a cobweb. He was right—nobody noticed it.

Halley's comet isn't seen while it is following the most distant part of its orbit, but careful measurements have shown how far it must travel into space. According to calculations, the comet swings out to about the distance of Pluto before it turns back toward the sun.

Although comets are occasionally destroyed or lost, Halley's again seems to be returning on schedule. On October 15, 1982, the comet was sighted a little over a billion miles away, following the right course to make a visit near the sun in 1986. That first sighting was made with the 200-inch reflecting telescope at Mount Palomar. In its basic design, the Hale telescope, as that remarkable instrument is called, is a mammoth copy of the tiny reflecting telescope Newton sent to the Royal Society. So Newton figured prominently in the event on two scores. The comet is named for Edmond Halley and the telescope for George Hale. But Newton's name might easily have been attached to either.

The Hale telescope pointing toward the North Star. (The adjustable mirror cover is in a closed-down position, concealing the mirror.)

9

First Approximation

After the publication of the *Principia*, Newton's law of gravity and his laws of motion were put to work to solve many problems both on earth and in the heavens. And for several centuries they were unquestioned. Some of his ideas may have needed clarification. Some of his own solutions may have been slightly off. But he seemed to have set a basis for solving all problems of motion for all objects large and small.

It turned out, however, that for objects very large and very small he hadn't quite succeeded. And it took another genius to discover why not.

The first hint that something might be lacking could be seen in the motion of Mercury, the closest planet to the sun. Like other planets, Mercury travels along an ellipse. If it were the only planet, Mercury would trace the same ellipse year after year. But the other planets act on Mercury to cause the direction of the ellipse to change little by little.

According to Newton's laws, that change in direction should amount to about a seventh of a degree per century. But measurements show a greater change. The measured change is 43 seconds of angle greater than predicted by Newton's laws—a difference of about 8 percent.

The first thought of astronomers, never suspecting Newton's laws, was that a small planet orbited the sun inside the orbit of Mercury. Such a speedy planet could cause the change they measured. And observers now and then thought they saw a dark object against the sun. But no planet could be discovered.

The explanation of Mercury's strange behavior didn't come until the twentieth century. And then it came from a man whose genius will always be compared with Newton's—Albert Einstein. With his theory of relativity Einstein showed that gravity doesn't quite follow Newton's law, especially near very heavy objects. Near the heavy sun, the inverse square law wasn't dead accurate. And so Mercury didn't behave quite as predicted. Using relativity, Einstein could explain the 43 seconds without help from a new planet.

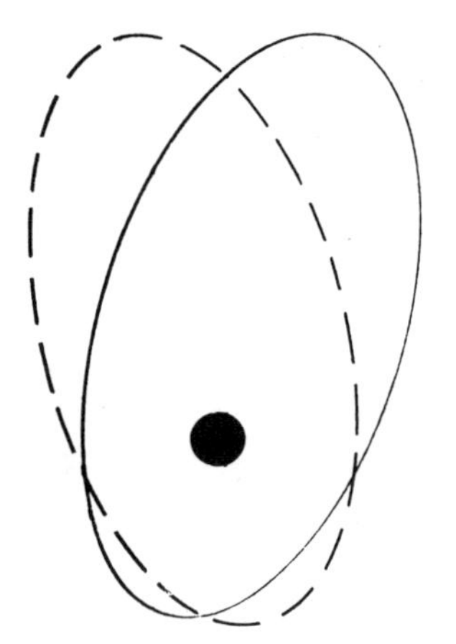

The change in the orbit of Mercury was imperfectly explained by Newton's laws.

Albert Einstein at the time when he was refining Newton's laws.

Einstein also found a problem with Newton's laws of motion. And that problem, it turned out, was most important for very small objects. The trouble wasn't with the laws so much as with the way they were used.

The usual way to use Newton's laws of motion is to assume that the mass of any object stays the same. If we pick up a ball and throw it, its mass doesn't change simply because we've set the ball in motion—or so we usually think. But Einstein showed that's not so. Any time you change the energy of an object, you change its mass. If you set a ball in motion, its mass increases.

For ordinary objects, the change in mass is so slight it can be ignored. The most careful measurement won't show it. It turns out that as long as the speed is small compared to the speed of light, there's no problem. But for very small objects—electrons, protons, atoms—the change in mass can be important. For with such small objects, speeds can be made very high.

Einstein did not upset Newton's laws, but he did put them in their place. Newton's law of gravity works beautifully as long as you're not too close to a very heavy object. And Newton's laws of motion work beautifully as long as your speeds are small compared to light. Newton's laws, though sometimes needing help from Einstein, are still very much alive.

In recent times Newton has been given a vote of confidence, if he needs one, by having a unit of force named after him. In SI units, which are now the standard units of scientists throughout the world, the unit of force is called the newton.

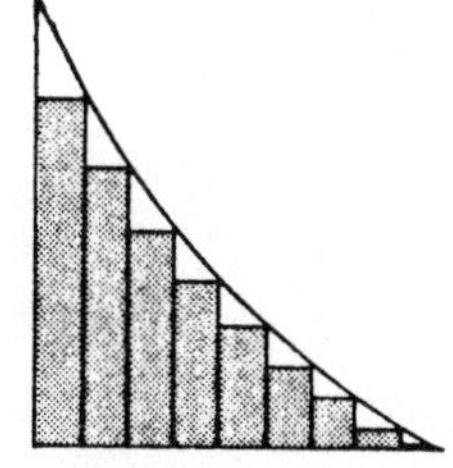

10

The Clash Over Calculus

The plague years, during which Newton had his first ideas about color and about gravity, are also supposed to be the time when he had his first ideas about calculus. The truth is that he probably had those ideas even earlier. But of the three "plague ideas," it was calculus that was the last to be publicized. Not until after the *Principia* did Newton's new approach to mathematics become known to the scientific public. By then, as it happened, another scientist had scooped him, disclosing an approach that did the same job.

Calculus is a technique of making an approximate answer exact by going to the limit. Suppose you want to find the speed of an object. You can measure the distance it has moved after a period of time and divide the distance by the time. But if the speed is changing, that gives only an approximate answer. To find the speed exactly, you have to cut the period of time down to practically nothing. Calculus is a technique for going to that limit—at least mathematically.

Calculus in its various forms is useful for finding slopes of curved lines, areas inside curves, and more. It has proved to be one of the most useful branches of mathematics.

After Newton invented calculus, he made no move to publicize his new methods. It was almost as though he wanted to keep them secret so that others wouldn't be able to solve the problems that he could now solve.

Even though he seemed reluctant to disclose his newfound knowledge, Newton did eventually let it be known that he had it. Without telling how he did it, he let his fellow scientists know just what sorts of problems he had learned to solve.

One of those scientists was a German named Gottfried Leibniz, a man of many talents. Lawyer, diplomat, historian, philosopher, Leibniz was a skilled mathematician as well. He answered Newton by suggesting that he too had developed ways to solve problems of the sorts Newton described.

The prospect that Leibniz might scoop him prodded Newton to some sort of action. But strangely, he did not simply reveal his methods. What he did was to write several sentences (in Latin) that would prove that he knew about the methods of calculus. He then simply reported the letters of the alphabet that he used in writing each sentence. For example, he reported that one of the sentences contained eleven *a*'s, one *b*, three *c*'s, and so on. His intention, of course, was that these counts of letters would be proof that he had written the sentences, when they were later disclosed.

Newton's "proof" was established rather late. He wrote his scrambled sentences a dozen years after his first thoughts about calculus. A copy of the letter that contained them reached Leibniz a few months later. Leibniz, recognizing that he would not easily learn about Newton's methods, decided then to disclose his own. In June of 1677 he wrote a long letter to the Royal Society showing in detail how his calculus worked.

Gottfried Leibniz.

The attitudes of the two scientists were curiously different. Leibniz was at heart a teacher, anxious to teach his fellow scientists how to solve new problems. Newton seemed happy to keep the rest of the scientific community in the dark. He gave the impression that it was just too much trouble to teach other scientists his methods. Not till many years later were his methods disclosed—and then in a book of a fellow scientist.

Although the methods of Newton and Leibniz could both be called calculus, they really looked quite different. The symbols were not at all alike, nor were the words. Even the way of developing the ideas was different. If you compared the work of the two men, you might easily decide that each had developed his methods by himself.

For some years there was no open dispute about who had invented calculus. Newton seemed confident that it was his invention made years before Leibniz appeared on the scene. He also seems to have had the feeling that Leibniz's invention—if it could be called that—may well have come from hints given by Newton. Leibniz seems to have had similar ideas about his own role. It was his calculus, he felt, and Newton had simply found a different way of expressing it.

A clash was probably inevitable. It took only the smallest incident to trigger it. In 1696, several years after Newton's methods had also been disclosed, Johann Bernoulli, a Swiss mathematician, proposed a problem for other scientists to solve. The problem can be stated in nonmathematical terms: If you design a frictionless chute to go between two points (one below and to the side of the other), what shape do you make it to give the quickest ride? Newton received the problem late one afternoon and solved it before he went to bed.

Newton suspected the problem was really a challenge from Leibniz, and he appears to have been right. A few years later Leibniz published the solution, boasting that it was only by his

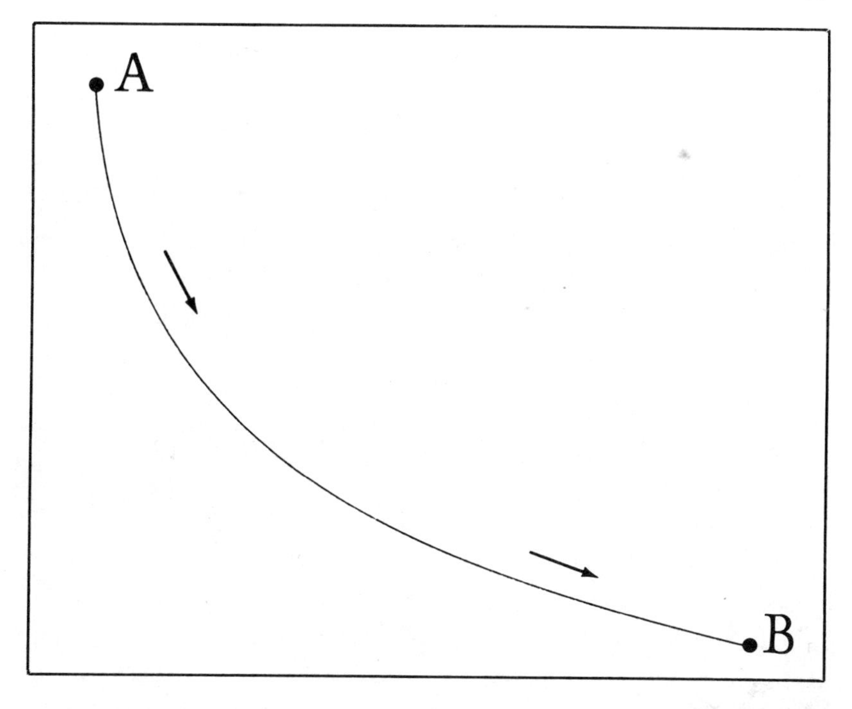

Johann Bernoulli's problem, which Newton quickly solved: What path gives the fastest run from A down to B with the help of gravity alone?

---

method of calculus that the problem had been solved. That naturally rankled Newton, for surely it was not Leibniz's method he had used, but his own.

The argument soon grew, helped along by friends of Newton or Leibniz. But there is good evidence that the two competitors themselves were active behind the scenes. Some of the charges were wild. Friends of Newton went so far as to suggest that Leibniz had deciphered Newton's scrambled sentences and gotten his ideas from that remarkable feat.

At one point a committee was formed by the Royal Society to investigate the truth. Since both Newton and Leibniz were Fellows of the society, it seemed a reasonable solution. But since Newton was then the president of the society and his faithful friend Halley one of the committee members, one has to be suspicious of their findings, which favored Newton.

The battle over the beginnings of calculus raged for years, cooled only by Leibniz's death in 1716. It remains a prime example of scientific infighting.

One result of the Newton-Leibniz dispute was a difference in the way calculus was used in England and on the Continent, even long after the central characters were dead. Scientists in England clung patriotically to Newton's symbols and words. Scientists on the other side of the English Channel followed Leibniz's lead.

The split lasted nearly a century, when it was mended in a fitting manner. A professor at Newton's own Cambridge University, with the help of some enthusiastic students, convinced English scientists that Leibniz had developed a more useful language for calculus.

But who really invented calculus? The majority view today is that both men invented it independently, Newton succeeding before his rival. But in the absence of any publication of his earliest ideas, how well Newton had succeeded could possibly be questioned.

Though Leibniz probably came up with his ideas later, you can easily argue that his ideas were better. With few exceptions it is Leibniz's symbols and words that are used to describe calculus today. The word "calculus" itself comes from Leibniz. Newton's word for the new branch of mathematics has been discarded along with his symbols. His word was "fluxions."

11

The Alchemist

If accomplishment always matched effort, Newton might be remembered today as an outstanding chemist. For over the years he probably spent more time in his small chemical laboratory than at any of his other pursuits.

Unfortunately, like other scientists of that time who spent hours mixing and brewing chemicals, Newton put his greatest effort into pursuing a will-o'-the-wisp. He tried long and hard to change one metal into another—lead, for example, into gold. In short, he was an alchemist.

Alchemy has a bad name today. And in truth it was often a mixture of science and mysticism. But the basic idea was sound. If everything is made of the same fundamental substances—which was only a guess then—it should be possible to transform one substance into another. What defeated the alchemists was that the transformation isn't so simple as they imagined it should be.

Although Newton wrote much about his chemical research, he published only one article of any consequence. The article, which appeared in 1701, probably some years after the work was done, wasn't about chemistry as such. In the work his aim was to discover the temperature of a coal fire or molten lead or the like—temperatures that might be of interest to a chemist.

Since neither Gabriel Fahrenheit nor Anders Celsius, nor anyone else that Newton was aware of, had yet invented a temperature scale, Newton invented his own. For his zero he chose the "heat of the winter air when water begins to freeze"—close to what the modern Celsius scale uses. As another point he selected body temperature "and that at which eggs are hatched," to which he gave a temperature of 12. That same temperature would later be used by Fahrenheit for his first temperature scale.

For measuring moderate temperatures Newton used a thermometer containing oil. But the most interesting feature of his work was the way he found temperatures that were too hot for his oil thermometer. He did it by measuring cooling time.

To find the temperature at which lead melts (and freezes), for example, he put a small piece of lead on a red-hot iron whose temperature was high enough to melt the lead. Then he placed the iron in a cool breeze.

Starting from the moment when the lead froze, Newton counted equal intervals of time as the iron cooled. When it was cool enough, he began measuring its temperature at those intervals with the oil thermometer.

Newton found that in equal times the difference in temperature between the iron and the air dropped equal fractions. If in one time interval the difference was cut in half, in the next it would be cut in half again.

If Newton assumed the earlier cooling followed the same pattern, he could then figure out the earlier temperatures of the iron. In this manner he decided that the melting point of lead on his scale was 96. It should have been 106, which isn't really far off, all considered.

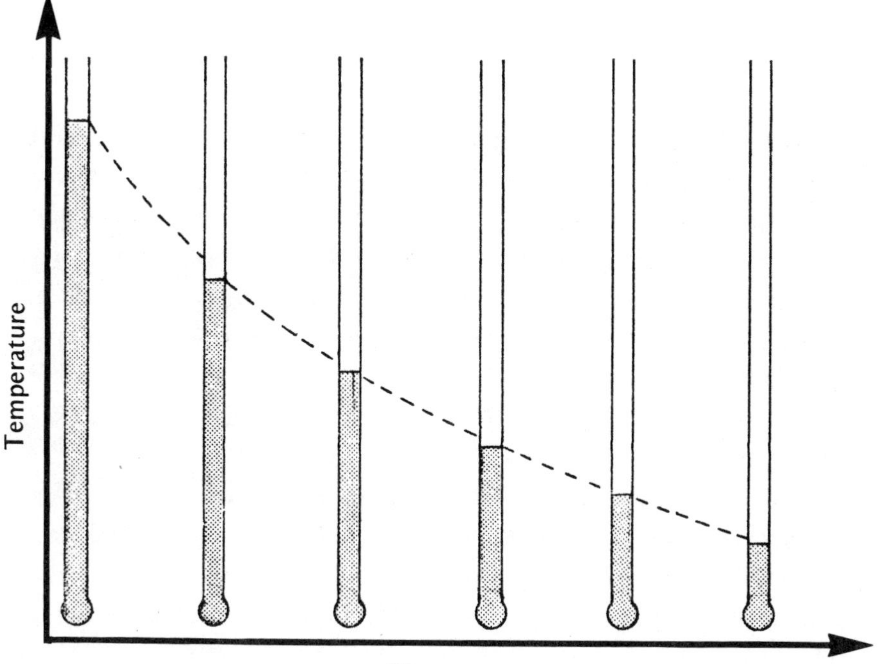

Newton discovered that the cooling of a heated object follows a simple mathematical law.

Newton's law of cooling has turned out to be a valuable idea. It is still used in talking about heat loss—at least as a first approximation. And the same idea solves problems in other areas. For example, like the warmth of Newton's red-hot iron, the radioactivity of a substance decreases by the same fraction in equal time intervals.

Newton's chemical hobby may have had a serious effect on his health. When he was about 50, he became quite ill. For about a year and a half his colleagues were unsure whether he would survive. Not only his body but his mind seemed to be affected.

Some suspected that it was a delayed reaction to the great effort of writing the *Principia* five years before. Others blamed his breakdown on depression over a fire that destroyed some of his writings.

But today the question is being raised whether he might simply have been suffering from mercury poisoning. Mercury was much used in alchemy, and its danger wasn't recognized at that time. Now we know that breathing its fumes, particularly over a period of time, can bring on illness and even death. In fact, it is now suspected that Charles II, an amateur chemist himself, may have died of mercury poisoning. His death came without explanation in 1685. A few years later, Newton may nearly have succumbed to the same poison.

Recent measurements of the mercury concentration in Newton's hair provide some support for this idea. One hair sample, probably from some years after his illness, shows forty times what is now considered a normal level of mercury.

Charles II.

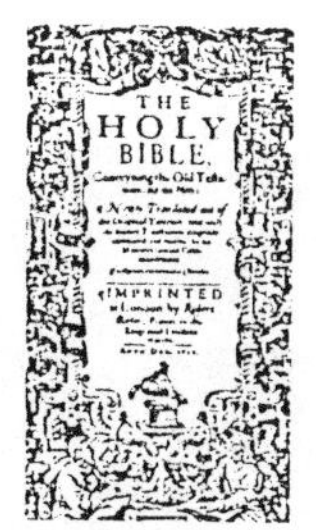

12

The Bible Student

Newton's life was notable for the number of strands of activity that ran through it. Work on light and motion and calculus, his most successful activities, began early and continued fitfully throughout his long life. Chemistry, exciting his interest before he left grade school, competed for his time for many years. Another interest that seems to have been as great and as long-lasting was religion.

In his nearly lifelong study of religion, Newton wrote well over a million words, mostly about the Bible, but with no intention, apparently, of publishing them. For as in science, his ideas in religion disagreed with some accepted views. And in religion as in science, he was anxious to avoid an argument. Beyond that, if his views on religion had become known, he could have lost his job. The religious climate that had made the early settlers of America desert England for a freer land was little changed by Newton's time.

But Newton's great interest in the Bible did lead to writings that were made public. Newton became intrigued with the problem of attaching dates to various events in ancient history.

The Bible provided a thread of history that went back to the Creation. And that thread, Newton felt, was one of our most accurate records of past times. In Newton's youth an Irish archbishop named Ussher had used the Bible to set the date of the Creation at 4004 B.C., and Newton found little reason to disagree.

Besides the Bible, Newton placed great faith in myths. The ancient gods and heroes of mythology, Newton decided, were all patterned after real people. And so another thread of history was spun by the ancient tales.

Agreeing or disagreeing with the tales of the Bible or mythology were the accounts of historians from earliest times. In Newton's view they were the least reliable source, too often rewriting history to make their country's past seem grander.

Newton also placed little faith in the findings of archaeologists, which were scanty in those days anyway. He sneered at what the "stone dolls" of ancient civilizations might show.

To weave the threads of history together to form an accurate sequence of dates, Newton, always the scientist, relied as much as he could on astronomy. For the heavens provide a convenient clock to measure the centuries.

The sun's place in the heavens on the first day of spring—the vernal equinox—changes slightly from year to year, for reasons Newton explained in the *Principia*. And so any record of the springtime location of the sun provides a good way to mark the century. Unfortunately, star maps, which commonly used the equinox as a point of reference, were drawn too rarely. And too often they were drawn by observers whose dates were unknown.

Publication of Newton's ideas came almost by accident. At her request, Newton supplied Princess Caroline, daughter of George I, with a short paper describing his ideas about the course of ancient history. It was intended to be a private paper, but somehow a copy of it made its way to France, where a

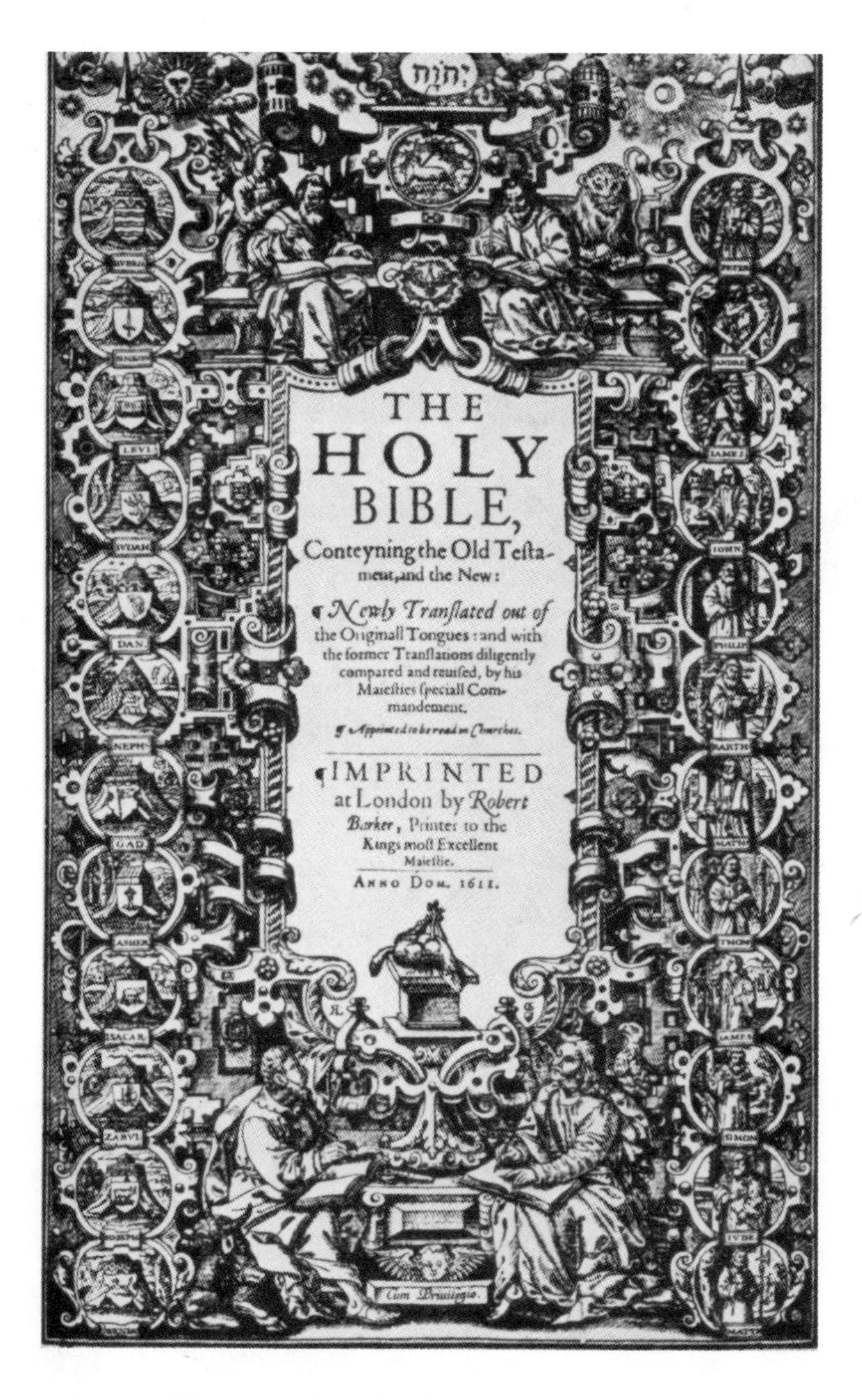

THE
HOLY
BIBLE,
Conteyning the Old Teſta-
ment, and the New:

Newly Tranſlated out of
the Originall Tongues: and with
the former Tranſlations diligently
compared and reuiſed, by his
Maieſties ſpeciall Com-
mandement.

Appointed to be read in Churches.

IMPRINTED
at London by *Robert*
Barker, Printer to the
Kings moſt Excellent
Maieſtie.

ANNO DOM. 1611.

Cum Priuilegio.

Title page of King James Bible of 1611.

publisher urged Newton to let him publish it, along with criticism from a French historian. When Newton failed to answer, he published the paper anyway.

So Newton was drawn into still another argument, now over the dates of antiquity. And this one survived longer than he did. His last thoughts on the subject were published after his death.

Coming from so great a mind, Newton's ideas had for a time great influence on the thinking about ancient history. Newton, though, is now little remembered for his careful historical work. Newer methods that rely on information that Newton either rejected or could not have known have made most of his answers useless, at least in the minds of modern historians.

A star map such as Newton used to nail down elusive dates.

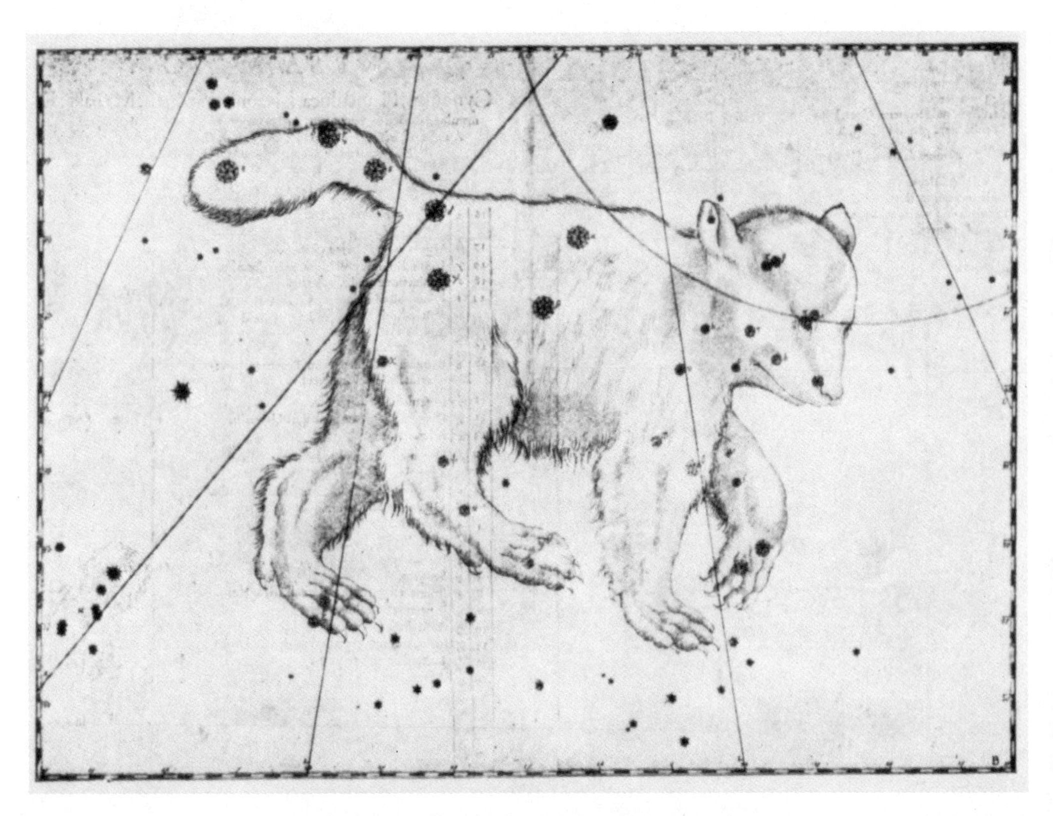

13

The Public Servant

The image of Newton as a loner who spent hours in his study or his laboratory working on topics ranging from chemistry to physics to mathematics to religion to ancient history is probably accurate. But after publication of the *Principia* the time spent on his various studies grew less. He seemed to hanker for a different life, a life that would not demand such taxing thought. Some have suggested that the illness of his early fifties ravaged his brilliant mind, but there is little evidence of that. He had simply grown weary, one can guess, of being a Cambridge scholar.

Newton's first significant brush with the world outside his academic circles came in 1687, the year the *Principia* was published. In that year James II, who had become king upon the death of his brother Charles II, attempted to have a Catholic monk admitted to Cambridge. Since by law no one could be admitted without swearing allegiance to the Church of England, Cambridge resisted the demands of the Catholic king.

The matter was brought to court, with the university represented by a group of nine university Fellows, including Newton.

Although Newton, no orator, had nothing to say during the public proceedings, in the private deliberations of the group he seems to have been the man who kept the university from bowing to the will of the king.

Soon after that incident, Newton agreed to run for Parliament and won a seat. There is no evidence that he enjoyed his experience as a lawmaker, which was brief. He is reported to have spoken only once, when he rose to ask that a window be closed. But he must have enjoyed the London scene. For he began to investigate the job opportunities in the London bureaucracy.

Newton's best contact in London was a man named Charles Montague, who had become a good friend of Professor Newton while a student at Cambridge. When Montague became Chancellor of the Exchequer, the chief money man in the government, he was able to wangle the job of Warden of the Mint for his brilliant friend. It was a job, suggested Montague, that paid well and required little work. Newton became Warden in 1696.

As it happened, for a while it was a rather busy job. Newton took over at the time of the Great Recoinage. British coins were then an awkward mixture of newer machine-made coins and older handmade coins. The older coins had lost value, both through wear and tear and through being filed or snipped. Montague had convinced Parliament that the old coins must be recalled and replaced with new ones. It was now Newton's job to manage the operation.

By reports, Newton was good at his new job. A few years later, after the recoinage was completed, the Master of the Mint died, and Newton was selected to fill that more exalted position. The job must have suited him, for he soon broke his ties with Cambridge. He had continued to hold his position as professor during his early years with the Mint, but now he saw no prospect of return. For the rest of his days he remained a London bureaucrat.

The Tower of London, which in Newton's time contained the Mint.

Since Newton was 53 when he joined the Mint, it sounds as if he took an early retirement from being a scientist. But the break with science was far from complete. During his years in London he played the role of scientist as well as public servant. The job of Warden had apparently kept him busy. But the job of Master seems to have given him time for other endeavors. It was during that time that he published his article on temperature measurement. He also wrote *Opticks*, a large effort.

His occupations as chemist, historian, and Bible scholar continued during his London years. And he continued, it seems, the absentminded ways of a deep thinker. A friend tells of visiting him to find a covered plate of food on the table. Growing impatient and hungry during the long wait for his host, the friend ate the food. Newton, when he finally appeared, lifted the cover to find the food gone. "Dear me," he is reported to have said, "I thought I had not dined, but I see I have."

Newton's London home from 1710 to 1725 (as it appeared in the mid-nineteenth century).

His continuing status as a scientist was emphasized by his election as president of the Royal Society in 1703, a post he would hold for the rest of his life. And it was surely for his brilliance as a scientist rather than as a bureaucrat that he was knighted in 1705. Although today it seems natural that any great British scientist will become a "Sir," Newton was the first to be so honored.

But if Newton remained a scientist, it was more as a promoter or publicizer than as a creator. Each week he presided over a meeting of the Royal Society, where he offered advice to the active scientists who performed their experiments or delivered their ideas. But he did not use those occasions to report research of his own.

Newton, in spite of his fame and position, had not grown into a genial elder scientist. It was during his London years that his battle with Leibniz over the invention of calculus was waged. He also had a tiff with John Flamsteed, an English astronomer.

Flamsteed was the first Astronomer Royal, which meant that he operated the newly created Royal Observatory at Greenwich. He had supplied Newton with lots of useful observations, especially of comets and of the moon, which Newton had used in writing Book III of the *Principia*.

But Flamsteed had held back many observations of the stars until they could be put in what he considered proper shape for publishing. After much urging, though, he had agreed to supply these figures if Newton promised not to publish them.

The end of the story was disagreeable. Somehow the promise was forgotten and the figures published. Worse, the man handling the publication was Edmond Halley, who was already genuinely hated by Flamsteed. After the publication, Flamsteed did his best to round up and destroy all the copies of the unauthorized catalog. And he added Newton to his list of enemies.

Sir Isaac Newton, age 67.

During most of his London years, bachelor Newton had a woman around the house. A niece, Catherine Barton, agreed to manage his home. According to reports, she was unusually attractive. Catherine herself seems to have been attracted to the men who handled Britain's money. She had a romance—perhaps even a secret marriage—with Charles Montague, the man who got Newton his position with the Mint, then eventually married the man who would fill Newton's job of Master after his death.

Living with a stunning niece probably brought more sociability to Newton than he might himself have drawn. Of course, his fame as a thinker brought many to his hearth to exchange thoughts with so great a genius. But Newton was never much of a talker and probably disappointed callers by his lack of brilliance in the drawing room.

Newton grew almost fat in the service of the government. His hair, turning gray early in his life, was snowy during his London years—but often covered by a wig. And though in Cambridge he was known for his untidiness of dress, in London he apparently reformed. A bureaucrat, unlike a university professor, must care a little about his appearance.

Newton spent very nearly as many years in London as he had in Cambridge. But in judging his contributions to science, you can throw away the London years without losing much. He added a little to what he had begun during his Cambridge years. Most of what attracted his attention in London, though, gave nothing of value to the world. But if Newton ever regretted the change in his lifestyle, he never said so.

For the sake of his health Newton deserted London for Kensington, a suburb west of town where the air was cleaner, a couple of years before he died. But in spite of his failing health, he still visited London often.

Early in March of 1727 he presided over his last meeting of the Royal Society. Two days later he became seriously ill. He died on March 20 at age 84. After lying in state for a time, Newton's body was buried in Westminster Abbey.

It did not decorate his tomb, but Newton himself may have uttered the best epitaph shortly before his death: "I do not know what I may appear to the world, but to myself I seem to have been only like a boy playing on the seashore, and diverting myself in now and then finding a smoother pebble or a prettier shell than ordinary, while the great ocean of truth lay all undiscovered before me."

As scientists continue to look for smoother pebbles and prettier shells, they still marvel at how many of them the premature child of a Woolsthorpe farmer was able to find.

Chronology

All dates refer to the "Old Style" calendar (although years are started with January 1, not March 25). The change to the "New Style" calendar in 1750, after Newton's death, added 10 or 11 days to the dates of Newton's time.

Year	Age	
1642	—	Born, December 25, in Woolsthorpe
1654	11	Entered the King's School in Grantham
1658	15	Quit school to farm in Woolsthorpe
1660	17	Returned to the King's School
1661	18	Entered Cambridge University as a subsizar at Trinity College
1665	22	Awarded bachelor's degree
		Retreated to Woolsthorpe because of the Great Plague; "the miraculous years"
1666	23	Returned to Cambridge
1668	25	Awarded master's degree
1669	26	Appointed Lucasian Professor of Mathematics at Cambridge

Year	Age	
1671	29	Reflecting telescope delivered to Royal Society
1672	29	Presented ideas on light and color to Royal Society; elected a fellow of Royal Society
1679	36	Wrote Hooke proposing a test to prove the earth's rotation
1687	44	*Principia* published
1689	46	Elected to Parliament
1693	50	Seriously ill
1696	53	Appointed Warden of the Mint; moved to London
1697	54	Solved Bernoulli's problem of quickest descent, promoting dispute with Leibniz over invention of calculus
1700	57	Appointed Master of the Mint
1701	58	Elected again to Parliament Resigned from Cambridge
1703	60	Elected president of the Royal Society
1704	61	*Opticks* published
1705	62	Knighted
1725	82	Moved to Kensington
1727	84	Died, March 20, in Kensington

Further Reading

The reader who would like to learn more about Newton will find a more detailed account of his life in the following books:

Anthony, H.D. *Sir Isaac Newton.* New York City: Abelard-Schuman, 1960.

Brewster, Sir David. *Memoirs of the Life, Writings, and Discoveries of Sir Isaac Newton.* Edinburgh, Scotland: Thomas Constable, 1855.

Dobbs, Betty Jo Teeter. *The Foundations of Newton's Alchemy.* Cambridge, England: Cambridge University Press, 1976.

Hall, A. Rupert. *Philosophers at War: The Quarrel Between Newton and Leibniz*. Cambridge, England: Cambridge University Press, 1980.

Lerner, Aaron B. *Einstein and Newton: A Comparison of the Two Greatest Scientists.* Minneapolis: Lerner Publishing Co.,1973.

Manuel, Frank E. *Isaac Newton, Historian*. Cambridge, Mass.: Harvard University Press, 1963.

More, Louis Trenchard. *Isaac Newton: A Biography.* New York City: Dover, 1962. (Republication of Scribner's, 1934.)

Sullivan, J.W.N. *Isaac Newton 1642-1727.* New York City: Macmillan, 1938.

Westfall, Richard S. *Never at Rest: A Biography of Isaac Newton.* Cambridge, England: Cambridge University Press, 1980.

Index